Corridor Rising

A decade of reinvestment following the 2008 floods

Rainbow over McGrath Amphitheatre (Calcam AP, LLC).

© Copyright 2018
Corridor Media Group

ISBN: 978-0-9828373-4-4

All rights reserved. No part of this work may be reproduced or copied in any form by any means, without written permission of the publisher.

Published by:
Corridor Media Group
2345 Landon Road, Suite 100
North Liberty, IA 52317

Publisher: John F. Lohman
Editor: Angela Holmes
Art Director: Susan Larson
Author: Gigi Wood

Project Manager: Andrea Rhoades
Nonprofit Profile Writers:
Annette Busbee, Steve Gravelle,
Angela Holmes

Special thanks: Judith Cobb,
Jane Lohman, Becky Lyons,
Adam Moore, Jean Suckow

Distributed by
Corridor Business Journal

Printed in the U.S.A. by NIS,
Davenport, IA.

Jacket printed in the U.S.A. by NIS,
Davenport, IA.

Leaders' Letter

Residents of the Corridor were met with one of the nation's worst natural disasters in history in June 2008. The 2008 Midwestern U.S. Floods impacted all our lives – flooding our homes, our businesses and our neighborhoods.

In the truest spirit of the Midwest, residents remained resolute before, during and after those unprecedented storms. Neighbors constructed sandbag walls, sheltered one another and helped each other rebuild. The Corridor is fortunate to be home to so many skilled and knowledgeable emergency responders and public servants, who diligently worked – and continue – to keep our communities safe.

From the moment the rain stopped, residents were in motion, tirelessly cleaning, rebuilding and planning the next steps of our recovery. Through steadfast dedication and hard work, along with ingenuity and an eye to the future, our communities were able to rebuild and evolve our assets to better withstand future challenges.

Ten years later, it is our honor to celebrate a stronger and more resilient world-class Corridor. On behalf of the cities and counties of the Corridor, we are pleased to present Corridor Rising, a tribute to the region's perseverance and renewal.

Kay Halloran
Cedar Rapids Mayor
2008

Jim Fausett
Coralville Mayor
2008
In memoriam

Sally Mason
University of Iowa President
2008

Regenia Bailey
Iowa City Mayor
2008

Brad Hart
Cedar Rapids Mayor
2018

John Lundell
Coralville Mayor
2018

Bruce Harreld
University of Iowa President
2018

Jim Throgmorton
Iowa City Mayor
2018

Third Street in downtown Cedar Rapids at sunset (William P. Buckets).

Table of Contents

Leaders' Letter 3

Introduction 13

Cedar River 16

Cedar Rapids 31

Iowa River 118

Coralville 124

University of Iowa 150

Iowa City 170

Index 198

A boy fishes along the Cedar River in Cedar Rapids (Greater Cedar Rapids Community Foundation).

Corridor Rising

Cedar Rapids Downtown Farmers' Market (William P. Buckets).

Family fun at the Cedar Rapids Downtown Farmers' Market (William P. Buckets).

Corridor Rising

Brucemore hosted Orchestra Iowa's post-flood comeback concert in the fall of 2008 to a standing-room-only crowd and continues to host it annually. Orchestra Iowa's home, the Paramount Theatre, was one of the downtown cultural landmarks flooded in 2008 (Orchestra Iowa/Visions Photography).

Above: *Sandbagging in downtown Cedar Rapids (Alliant Energy).*

Opposite, left: *A sandbag wall in downtown Cedar Falls (Don Poggensee).*

Opposite, right: *Emergency personnel rescue pets from homes in Cedar Rapids (Alliant Energy).*

Introduction

Eastern Iowa was forever altered in June 2008 when massive flooding breached levees and dams throughout the region. Busy streets became rivers, homes were destroyed and the state's largest university was submerged. Daily life stopped as residents watched and waited for the water to recede.

Thankfully, no lives were lost in the Eastern Iowa storms, although the 2008 Midwestern U.S. Floods remain among the top 20 costliest natural disasters in United States history, with more than $11.5 billion in damages. The hardest-hit cities in Iowa were Cedar Rapids, Iowa City, Coralville and their surrounding communities, with a combined total of $6.6 billion in damage.

While the devastation was shocking, what made the disaster truly remarkable was the way communities came together to protect, clean and rebuild their neighborhoods. Eastern Iowa residents filled and placed more than 30 million sandbags before the waters rose. During the flood, the community reacted swiftly, with emergency responders traveling by boat to rescue neighbors and save as much of the region's basic infrastructure as possible. As it continued to rain, volunteers rolled up their sleeves and stepped in, rescuing nearly 200 patients from a community hospital and helping more than 10,000 people escape their homes when the water rose higher than expected.

Neighbors and businesses returned day after day to assist with cleanup and repairs. Later, the work shifted to recovery, and the communities began to rebuild.

They did more than replace what was lost, however. More than $1 billion was invested in state-of-the-art business, cultural, housing and campus facilities. Public officials, corporate leaders and neighborhoods partnered to improve, modernize and reshape neighborhoods and business districts, resulting in population and economic growth, as well as increased amenities.

"You would not wish a disaster on any community, but it did create generational change in Cedar Rapids," said Pat Deignan, market president of Bankers Trust. "Things happened here that would not have happened for a generation. And it only happened because of the crisis. In a crisis, you step in and make things happen because you have to."

This book commemorates the flooding of 2008 and celebrates the subsequent recovery, focusing on how cities and businesses worked together to create a stronger Eastern Iowa Corridor.

The numbers and estimates provided in this publication are just that – estimates. Much of the flooding impact cannot be quantified. Some families left their homes after the flood, never to be heard from again. Small businesses lost more than what could be reported. The intrinsic value of artifacts, library books, art collections and other valuables can never be counted. The emotional strain and trauma of the floods can never be adequately depicted. The thousands of volunteers who sandbagged and later, hosted evacuated families, can never be thanked enough. What this publication does aim to capture, though, is the incredible recovery efforts that continue to this day.

Top: *Flooding in downtown Cedar Rapids (Alliant Energy).*

Above: *A&W Restaurant flooding (Alliant Energy).*

Opposite: *Top, residents explore a flooded neighborhood (City of Cedar Rapids). Bottom, floodwaters overtake Highway 30 (City of Cedar Rapids). Right, vehicles merging onto Interstate 380 to evacuate the area (City of Cedar Rapids).*

Comparing the 'great floods'

People unfamiliar with Iowa may not realize that it's much more than a state between two rivers, the Missouri and Mississippi. Dozens of waterways traverse the state, and flooding is a familiar event for many residents.

It's not uncommon for many to cite the Great Flood of 1993 as Iowa's most significant natural disaster. Back then, all 99 Iowa counties were declared federal disaster areas. Seventeen people died and more than 10,000 people were evacuated from their homes that year. It rained for 130 consecutive days, causing more than $2.7 billion ($4.5 billion adjusted for inflation) in damage.

In Iowa, 80 of the state's 99 counties received federal disaster declarations from the Federal Emergency Management Agency (FEMA), while 86 of the counties received state disaster declarations. More than $10 billion in damage was caused statewide. Two people in Western Iowa died in the disaster. Approximately 40,000 people were affected and more than 10,000 were evacuated from their homes. Heavy snowfall and spring rains from December 2007 to May 2008, followed by weeks of thunderstorms

INTRODUCTION

in late May and June caused the flooding.

While it's difficult to sufficiently compare the two flooding events, there is one striking difference. The Great Flood of 1993 set the record for high water throughout the state. In 1993, the Cedar River in Cedar Rapids crested at 19.27 feet; in 2008 it peaked at 31.12 feet. The Iowa River in Iowa City crested at 28.52 feet in 1993; in 2008 it reached a height of 31.53 feet.

Many improvements – such as enhanced levees and pump stations – had been installed since 1993, so many in fact, no one expected 2008's flooding to result in higher water levels and more severe damage. When 2008 waters rose 11 feet above the highest level in Cedar Rapids' history, no one was fully prepared.

> "YOU WOULD NOT WISH A DISASTER ON ANY COMMUNITY, BUT IT DID CREATE GENERATIONAL CHANGE IN CEDAR RAPIDS. THINGS HAPPENED HERE THAT WOULD NOT HAVE HAPPENED FOR A GENERATION," SAID PAT DEIGNAN, MARKET PRESIDENT OF BANKERS TRUST IN CEDAR RAPIDS

Cedar Rapids under water in June 2008 (Alliant Energy).

Lightning over Veterans Memorial Building in Cedar Rapids (William P. Buckets).

Saturated earth across the river basin

The period between December 2007 and May 2008 was the second wettest in U.S. history, with the greatest amount of precipitation falling along the Mississippi River basin, which includes Minnesota, Iowa, Wisconsin, Illinois and Missouri.

Iowa communities along the Cedar and Iowa rivers experienced a winter of heavy snowfall, followed by a spring of unceasing rains, resulting in saturated earth and swollen rivers. Then, for a few weeks in May, the rain stopped. When residents thought the worst was over, three weeks of thunderstorms began throughout the region, creating the second wettest June since weather records began.

Up to 12 inches of rain fell each day as storms moved through Iowa, Missouri, Illinois, Wisconsin, Ohio and Michigan. By mid-June, levees across the Midwest had been breached and dams overflowed, creating some of the worst flooding the country had ever experienced. In Iowa, 80 of the state's 99 counties received federal disaster declarations from the Federal Emergency Management Agency (FEMA).

Tom Aller, then president of Alliant Energy's Iowa utility, began watching the rainfall long before the worst hit Cedar Rapids. The power company is headquartered in Madison, Wisconsin, and serves a three-state region: Iowa, Minnesota and Wisconsin. Alliant's subsidiary, Interstate Power and Light Co., is based in Cedar Rapids, and from his office there, Aller was watching storms in northwest Iowa and southern Minnesota closely.

"There was a lot of heavy rainfall in Minnesota – you could see what was coming," he said. "But we couldn't prepare for something like this. It was so wet, we couldn't send our people out to work with the downed power lines. When you can't get a truck in a ditch safely, you can't fix downed power lines and poles."

The utility would later have much greater challenges.

An unstable air mass moved into the Midwest on May 22-31, bringing with it thunderstorms and tornadoes, including a deadly E5 in Parkersburg.

The weather system migrated east to Mason City, where 4 inches of rain fell in early June, pushing the Winnebago River to record flood levels. More than 200 businesses were forced to evacuate, flooding many. A railroad bridge washed out; the city's water treatment plant was flooded and the wastewater treatment facility came within 4 inches of flooding. Since then, several flood walls and other improvements have been constructed to help protect the city from future flood events.

Rains continued south and east across the state, inundating the northern end of the Cedar River basin at Charles City on June 9. At least 500 houses were flooded. Two historic landmarks were affected: A Frank Lloyd Wright home experienced $1 million in damage, and the community's beloved 1906 suspension bridge was destroyed. Overall, the community experienced roughly $20 million in flood damage.

Further down river in Waverly, the river crested at 19.33 feet, nearly 3 feet higher

than the previous record set in 1999. About 500 homes and businesses flooded and 1,000 were without power on June 10.

That same day, flooding reached Waterloo and Cedar Falls, where it suddenly increased in flow, overwhelming lift stations and washing away a portion of a railroad bridge. Homes, businesses and infrastructure sustained $20 million in damage.

Roughly 40 miles downriver, the city of Vinton achieved historic flood levels June 10-11. On June 11, a 15-block area was flooded and the city lost power after floors collapsed at the auxiliary power plant. Kirkwood Community College's Vinton site was evacuated June 9 and flooded June 11, filling with 18 inches of water. A temporary facility was opened June 23 at the local middle school. After cleanup, sanitation and renovation, the Kirkwood site reopened for students Aug. 19.

"When the flood went through Cedar Falls and Waterloo, it really wasn't much of an event, then that night, it rained 5 inches, so there wasn't much time to do much to prepare," said Mick Starcevich, Kirkwood Community College's president who retired in June 2018.

Above: *Lewis Access Road near NextEra Energy in Palo (NextEra Energy).*

Opposite: *Town of Palo under water (NextEra Energy).*

Flooding arrives in Palo

All 890 residents of Palo, located just northwest of Cedar Rapids, were evacuated before the flood arrived June 11. There was more than $30 million in damage to homes, businesses and city facilities.

The town's focal point, the Palo City Hall and Community Center, housed the town's library, educational center, senior center and gymnasium. The center flooded and because of the depth of the water throughout the city, water could not be pumped out for 10 days. The center was filled with what is known as "black water" – rainfall contaminated with pollutants and chemicals – for so long, the building was razed. A new, stormproof center was rebuilt in 2011 in a safer location.

"Palo was under water," said Linn County Supervisor John Harris, a 20-year resident of the city. "Speaking from a small-town perspective, I'm still living in Palo. I'm still in the house that was flooded in 2008 … even my house is more flood-protected than it was then. We're just all smarter than we were then."

The Palo Mini-Mart, the town's only convenience store, was also flooded. The building was positioned in a shallow area of town, so the owner was able to elevate the site 8 feet and rebuild. He reopened in two months.

The new community center and convenience store are important resources to the 550 employees at the nearby NextEra Energy Duane Arnold Energy Center, a nuclear power plant that generates enough electricity to power 600,000 homes annually. The

generation plant, located along the Cedar River, did not flood and remained operational throughout the event.

"Where the water crested, we could have continued to operate even if it would have come up 5 more feet, which would be an incredible amount of water. This flood got to 752 feet (above sea level) and we can operate until 757," said Dean Curtland, the power plant's site director.

As flood waters inundated power plants along the Cedar River, Duane Arnold was able to provide Alliant Energy with a reliable power source.

"What a number of people don't realize is, because power plants are always built by a source of water, we were basically the only power plant in the eastern third of Iowa that wasn't impacted, that was able to stay at full power," Curtland said. "So, we were very important to the grid at that time."

As the flood situation worsened, city and county emergency management officials gathered at Kirkwood Community College in Cedar Rapids to review disaster plans and create strategies to keep residents safe.

Seasoned experts at disaster planning, the nuclear plant staff undergoes extensive preparations, planning and drills several times a year. Because of this, the power plant's emergency management team was sent to Kirkwood to partner with area emergency management officials to help with the region's disaster response plans.

A report released in August 2012 by the National Academy of Sciences recognized NextEra Energy Duane Arnold Energy Center for that partnership, which the academy said was responsible for the lack of fatalities during the flood. During a flood event of 2008's magnitude, deaths of up to 70 people are expected. Instead, no lives were lost and 10,000 people were evacuated successfully.

"OUR EMERGENCY PLANNING WAS ALWAYS GOOD, BUT DURING THE FLOOD IT BECAME NEXT LEVEL. IT'S TRULY A PARTNERSHIP AND IT SERVES THE COMMUNITY REALLY, REALLY WELL," SAID DEAN CURTLAND, SITE DIRECTOR AT NEXTERA ENERGY DUANE ARNOLD ENERGY CENTER.

"The evacuation worked so well because of that partnership," Curtland said.

About 20 percent of NextEra's workforce was affected by the flood. Most roads leading to the facility were washed out that June, making the power plant difficult to reach. Many employees stayed on site, working 12-hour shifts to ensure the facility continued to operate.

After the waters receded, 30 employees were sent to Palo every day for months to help with cleanup and recovery. That work inspired NextEra employees to start a companywide charitable-giving organization that to this day contributes year-round to the community.

Opposite, top: *NextEra Energy mechanics traveling by boat in Palo (NextEra Energy).*

Opposite, bottom: *Maintenance and security crews monitor flooding near the NextEra Energy Duane Arnold Energy Center (NextEra Energy).*

Above, top to bottom: *The Benton County Law Enforcement Center in Vinton, completed in 2011 after flooding destroyed the previous facility (Jeff Holmes).*

The Palo Mini Mart was elevated and rebuilt after the 2008 floods (Jeff Holmes).

The newly constructed Palo Community Center and City Hall (Jeff Holmes).

Farmland, government buildings damaged in Linn County

In rural areas, the flood was catastrophic for the agriculture industry. Heavy precipitation during winter and spring months delayed planting for most farmers. Statewide, nearly 3 million acres, or 50 percent, of corn and soybeans were flooded in June 2008. Stagnant water sat in fields, sometimes for weeks, exacerbating the effects of the flood.

Storage and transportation of crops slowed, as many bins and roads were impaired. Soybean crushing plants, agricultural processing facilities and milling plants were closed or operating at reduced capacity during, and for weeks after, the flood. Throughout the state, thousands of livestock died. In Linn County, 86 farms were flooded.

Below: *A farm flooded in rural Benton County (Jeff Holmes).*

Opposite, top: *Flooded railroad cars in Linn County (City of Cedar Rapids).*

Opposite, bottom: *Aerial view of Cedar Rapids flooding (City of Cedar Rapids).*

Many Linn County government buildings and services were also affected by the high water. Ten county buildings, including the jail, courthouse, administrative offices and sheriff's department, were damaged, causing more than $60 million in damage. The courthouse and jail, which are located on May's Island, in the middle of the Cedar River, were flooded to the second floor.

"It was the perfect storm of rising water and record rainfall and it was just unbelievably devastating," Harris said.

After the flood, the county installed tiling and pumps to improve protection for its buildings. Some were demolished, others were moved out of the flood zone and a few were sold and redeveloped.

The Linn County Courthouse was renovated and improved with a new skywalk to improve flood protection. The project cost $8 million.

The Community Services Building of Linn County, which hosts human services departments, was moved far west of the river. It was rebuilt for $16.3 million and reopened in 2011, receiving silver LEED (Leadership in Energy and Environmental Design) certification for its environmental sustainability. County buildings were constructed using funding from grants, state and federal sources and recovery bonds.

"There were many lessons learned from the flood, like don't put your HVAC (heating, ventilation and air conditioning) systems in the basement and don't store records in the basement in flood-prone areas," Harris said. "If we were to experience a flood now to 2008 levels, we would be in pretty good shape."

The county has updated its disaster plan with action plans for various stages of flooding.

"Our flood action plan tells us exactly what happens when the river gets to 14 feet and when it gets to 18 feet, these areas need attention," he said. "We know how to react to each flood stage, what to attend to and how to prepare."

Since the flood, more residents have moved to the county and additional businesses have opened.

"We are always growing both residentially and commercially and we're growing into those places that weren't impacted in 2008," Harris said.

"WE KNOW HOW TO REACT TO EACH FLOOD STAGE, WHAT TO ATTEND TO AND HOW TO PREPARE," SAID LINN COUNTY SUPERVISOR JOHN HARRIS.

Opposite: *Mays Island flooding (Alliant Energy).*

Above: *Central Fire Station flooded (City of Cedar Rapids).*

Top: *Buses navigate through Cedar Rapids flooding (Alliant Energy).*

Corridor Rising

Downtown Cedar Rapids, including May's Island and the main bridges, was underwater June 13, 2008. (City of Cedar Rapids?)

Cedar Rapids the hardest hit in Iowa

Cedar Rapids was undoubtedly the hardest hit community in Iowa during the 2008 floods. On June 13 – Friday the 13th – the Cedar River crested at 31.12 feet, more than 11 feet higher than the previous record in 1993.

Cherished photos and mementos, as well as important business documents and equipment, were placed on the top shelves of bookcases and filing cabinets at buildings in the flood's path. Yet when the worst of the flood hit, some homes filled with as much as 12 feet of water. Most businesses had 8 feet. At a flooded downtown deli, loaves of bread were found stuck to the ceiling tiles.

Historic neighborhoods were gutted. The Time Check, Czech Village, Kingston Village and surrounding neighborhoods were under mandatory evacuation orders, as gas and electricity to those homes were shut off. Everyone left safely, but 5,900 houses flooded. Most evacuees stayed with family, friends and in hotels while they waited for city crews to inspect their homes for structural damage. The city later acquired 1,375 properties for $147.3 million with federal,

Aerial view of downtown Cedar Rapids flooding (Alliant Energy).

state and local funds to remove residents from the floodplain.

Downtown, streets turned into rivers, destroying businesses and cultural landmarks. More than 450 companies flooded and 1,360 jobs were lost. Major manufacturers, such as Cargill Corn Milling, Quaker Oats, Archer Daniels Midland and Penford Products were flooded, affecting about 3,000 workers. A downtown fixture since 1889, iconic furniture store Smulekoff's flooded, with some reporting that couches shot out of the building as the river's current overtook the building.

Among the many arts and cultural organizations affected were the African-American Museum of Iowa, Cedar Rapids Public Library, Cedar Rapids Museum of Art, Orchestra Iowa, Freedom Festival office, Girl Scouts of Eastern Iowa and Western Illinois, Indian Creek Nature Center, Iowa Art Works, Legion Arts/CSPS, National Czech & Slovak Museum and Library, New Bohemia Group, Paramount Theatre, Science Station, Theatre Cedar Rapids and YMCA.

Hundreds of city and county buildings were flooded, including several major city buildings: City Hall, the central fire station, animal control, public works and city bus terminal. The U.S. Federal Courthouse was destroyed.

Three of four collector wells and 46 vertical wells were disabled, limiting clean water for drinking and bathing.

Right: *A vehicle tries to make its way through flooded streets (Alliant Energy).*

Opposite: *The Cedar River floods the streets of downtown Cedar Rapids (Don Becker, U.S. Geological Survey).*

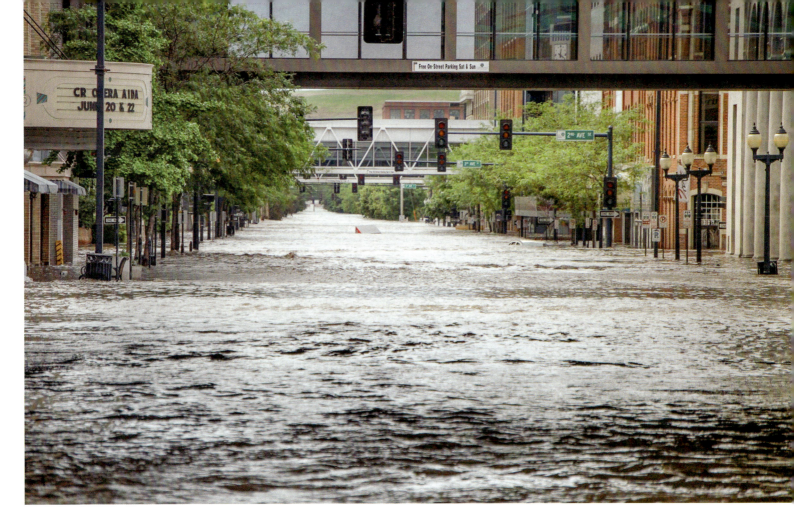

In the middle of the night June 13, Mercy Medical Center evacuated 176 patients as officials worried the hospital's backup generator would be flooded. Patients were moved to other health care facilities in the area. After the hospital was cleaned and tested for safety, it reopened patient services in phases starting June 16.

Overall, the damage in Cedar Rapids was extensive. The flood swamped 10 square miles, displacing 10,000 people. Damage totaled more than $6 billion. At the time, the 2008 Midwestern U.S. Floods was the nation's worst flooding disaster, second only to Hurricane Katrina, just a few years earlier.

During the days and weeks leading up to the flood, residents filled and placed more than 3 million sandbags to protect neighborhoods and businesses near the Cedar River. As waters continued to rise, volunteers showed up daily to add additional layers of sandbags. Yet the river continued to go up, much faster and with a much more powerful current than expected – and the most essential infrastructure began to break down.

Water overtook important roadways up and down the Cedar River during the flooding. Ellis Boulevard was closed on June 9, followed by Edgewood Road on June 10. As the rivers crested, several bridges throughout the region closed, as well as portions of interstates 380 and 80 on June 13. U.S. Highway 30 and state highways 1 and 13 were also closed.

Some detours sent drivers up to two hours out of their way, and the Iowa Department of Transportation asked commercial truck drivers to avoid the state completely. Many railroad tracks were submerged and several railroad bridges were washed away.

And then the power went out.

"WE'RE WELL POSITIONED BECAUSE WE HAVE A DIVERSE ECONOMIC BASE. I THINK WE ARE IN A VERY COMPETITIVE POSITION WITH MANUFACTURING, AGRICULTURE, HIGH TECHNOLOGY AND LOGISTICS," SAID LES GARNER, PRESIDENT AND CEO, GREATER CEDAR RAPIDS COMMUNITY FOUNDATION.

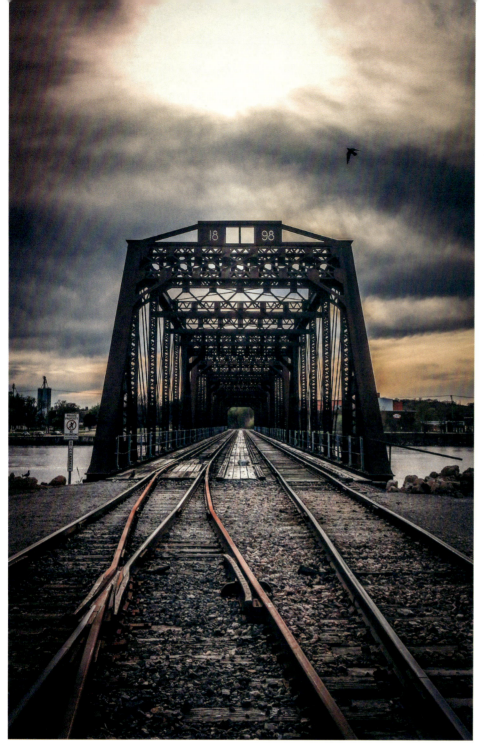

Top left: *Railroad bridge at the Quaker Oats plant (William P. Buckets).*

Bottom left: *Debris floating down the Cedar River (Alliant Energy).*

Above: *A twisted railroad bridge in Cedar Rapids (Alliant Energy).*

"IT'S UNBELIEVABLE HOW FAST DOWNTOWN CEDAR RAPIDS CAME BACK. YOU HAVE TO GIVE CREDIT TO THE SUPPORT FROM THE CITY AND TO OTHER COMMUNITIES THAT WERE HELPFUL," SAID DOUG KOPP, SENIOR VICE PRESIDENT OF OPERATIONS AND PRESIDENT OF ALLIANT ENERGY'S IOWA UTILITY.

Above: *Flooding at Alliant Tower, Alliant Energy's Cedar Rapids headquarters (Alliant Energy).*

Opposite: *Alliant Energy's generating station (Alliant Energy).*

The power goes out

On June 12, Alliant Energy decided to shut down operations as water began to overtake its power plant and other facilities. The choice was difficult for the company and its employees but was required to maintain safety.

"When there is a natural disaster, it usually means that Mother Nature has torn the system up and [utility crews] go out and put it back up and restore power to the customers," said Dee Brown, director, customer operations for the Iowa west region. "In the case of the flood, they were purposely shutting the power off for safety reasons, and that was hard for them as they knew it impacted customers."

At the time, Brown was in charge of Alliant's electrical operations in Cedar Rapids and was working at the company's Shaver Road facility. Crews worked for days trying to maintain power at the facility and protect the plant from floodwaters, but were eventually forced to evacuate.

"As we left, it was obvious that we had waited almost too long to leave," she recalled. "Water was up to the cabs on large trucks as we exited Shaver Road. We could not get under the interstate, so we went up the off ramp."

It was a similar situation at the company's Sixth Street plant, where Doug Kopp worked at the time. Kopp now serves as senior vice president of operations and president of Alliant Energy's Iowa utility.

"I first got to the Sixth Street plant at 5 in the morning and there was a little bit of water in the parking lot," he said. "An hour later, we were told we needed to get our vehicles to higher ground."

He stepped outside to check on weather conditions.

"It was dark out, and when the lightning would flash, there was water as far as the eye could see," he said.

The decision was made to evacuate the plant.

"The water was rising, at that point, 8 to 12 inches an hour," Kopp said. "The plant

had shut down – plants are usually loud with the equipment – but that sound wasn't there. The alarm was sounding and the lightning was flashing."

The next step was to announce the evacuation to the crew.

"Power plant guys are some of the toughest characters around, because their jobs are so tough sometimes," he said. "Usually, when they walk in, there's some chatter, but you could hear a pin drop that morning. Everybody's wet and we're sitting there and the water's rushing into the basement at an enormous rate, just pouring in."

He told them they had 30 minutes to finish up their work.

"Some of those guys, they had worked there 30, 35 years," he said. "It was really a hard moment. No one wanted to give up the fight. They had shut down the plant, but that equipment stays hot. You could hear popping in the basement when cold water hit hot equipment. They did some great work focusing on what they needed to, and then we sounded the alarm again because I was afraid they wouldn't leave, that they would keep working. I said, 'OK, we're done, I want everybody out.' And we were able to wade out; the water was about 2 feet deep."

Alliant's Tom Aller, who had been watching storms move across southern Minnesota and northern Iowa for weeks, was at the company's main office in downtown Cedar Rapids, a block from the Cedar River. He had worked for weeks on disaster

planning and coordinating the response to storms upstream. Then it arrived in Cedar Rapids.

"We lost our entire operation, all of our facilities," said Aller, who was the company's top Cedar Rapids executive at the time and has since retired. "We watched all of our equipment float down the river – poles, trucks, transformers, even bulbs and dials."

Alliant employees were evacuated and moved to space at Kirkwood Community College's Training and Outreach Services campus, where several other flooded businesses set up shop. Alliant crews immediately began mobilizing in Cedar Rapids to restore power, while other teams raced south to the city of Burlington to respond to impending floods.

Aller and his team held daily briefings to inform the city, residents and business community of progress. Meeting notes were taken with pencil and paper. The utility's call center had flooded and within a few days customer inquiries were rerouted. There was no way to communicate with crew members working in the field.

"Everyone wanted to know when the power would come back on," Aller said. "No one could do their job until we did our job and restored power."

As temporary and permanent power systems came online, utility crews often

Opposite: *Alliant Energy trucks submerged by floodwaters (Alliant Energy)*

Above: *Alliant Energy workers make flood repairs (Alliant Energy).*

needed to turn on one house at a time.

"Crews worked with city officials to do inspections as water was receding, to try to help customers get back into their homes," Brown said. "Our crews were allowed into areas before residents were. This put an emotional toll on crews, as customers asked them for information about the condition of their homes."

Downtown, businesses and houses were powered by a steam tunnel system that had flooded. Alliant began working on a temporary steam system to ensure buildings had working heat by winter.

Backup generators were used at many buildings downtown until power was restored July 3.

"We were one of the first lights back on downtown," Kopp said.

Surrounding neighborhoods were without power for a few days after the flood. However, some homes and businesses were so damaged, power could not be restored until interior electrical systems were rebuilt or repaired, and then inspected by the city.

Eventually, Alliant decommissioned and demolished its Sixth Street plant and steam system. After the flood, the utility repaired and improved its Cedar Rapids infrastructure. Alliant constructed a new substation to help power the community, moved equipment to higher ground, improved its technology and revised its disaster planning for future events.

"Looking back, we were fortunate to have leaders whose overarching goal was to work together to make things better," Aller said. "People talked and communicated; everybody worked together. I don't think I ever saw that break down."

Above: *Banners announced Alliant Energy's return to operation downtown (Alliant Energy).*

Opposite: *Alliant Tower at night (William P. Buckets).*

Downtown Cedar Rapids is illuminated at night (William P. Buckets).

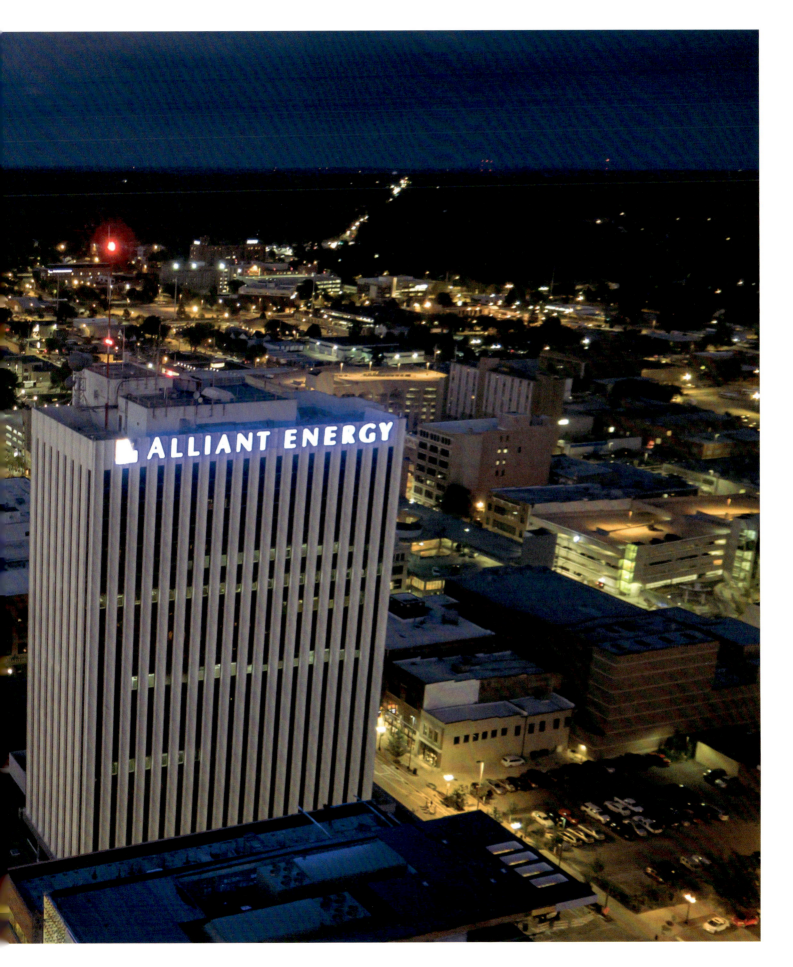

Flood response a 24/7 job

"THERE'S ALWAYS A SILVER LINING IN SAD STORIES. AND THE SILVER LINING, IN MY OPINION, WAS IT REALLY CAUSED CEDAR RAPIDS AND IOWA CITY TO REIMAGINE WHO THEY COULD BE," SAID BARRY BOYER, FORMER PRESIDENT AND CEO, VAN METER INC.

Alliant Energy was one of many companies operating 24 hours a day, seven days a week to prepare and respond to the flood.

Van Meter Inc., a wholesale electrical distributor, sells much of the equipment businesses need to function, such as light bulbs, wiring and conduit, circuits, fuses and generators. During the weeks leading up to the flood, the company ordered millions of dollars of extra inventory to help its commercial and industrial customers if the flood turned out to be extreme.

"We were horrified by the potential flooding we faced," said Barry Boyer, then president and CEO of Van Meter. "We put all of our manufacturers on notice that we had an impending disaster and we told them we may need orders within a day or two. And we stayed open 24/7 to help customers."

It was all hands-on deck as the flood worsened.

"I was up in Wisconsin at our sister company, Werner. Waters were rising, it was beginning to flood [in Cedar Rapids]. They knew it was going to be bad, but they didn't know how bad it was going to be at that point," said Mike Gassmann, Van Meter's chief growth officer. "I was at a training meeting and I got a call from Barry sometime in the late morning. And he said, 'Mike, do you know what's happening to our city?' And I remember stepping out and talking to him and he said, 'our city is flooding, it's getting destroyed.' So, I left training and headed back, not knowing what I was going to see. My home is in Marion and I told my wife, 'I'm not going to come home right now, I need to drive downtown and go to the office and see what's happening.' I was talking to my mom when I drove down the single lane of I-380 south and I couldn't talk because I was choking up, I started crying. I'll never forget that time, just looking over the interstate."

As floodwaters began to recede, company leaders visited several manufacturing plants to determine what equipment was needed to get them up and running.

"I went to Diamond V with Barry Boyer and it was dark; rain was coming in," said Dave Klostermann, a Van Meter customized solutions manager. "He would hold a

Opposite and above: *Van Meter Inc. employee-owners fill and place sandbags around a house in Cedar Rapids (Van Meter Inc.).*

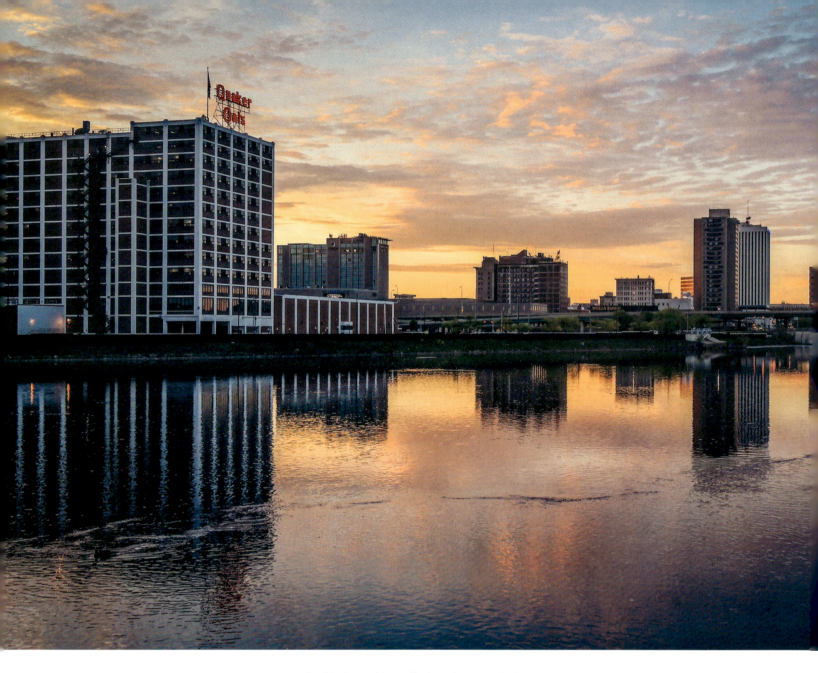

Above: *Ducks swim past the Quaker Oats factory along the Cedar River (William P. Buckets).*

Opposite: *Van Meter Inc.'s headquarters in Cedar Rapids (Van Meter Inc.).*

flashlight and list off what they needed and I took notes with a pencil."

Van Meter employees conducted several similar walk-throughs of flooded businesses.

"The Quaker Oats sign is a very visible thing in our community, and I remember when we were meeting with their leaders, they were bound and determined that the light would be turned back on as a symbol of, 'we're here, we're staying here and it's going to be powered up,'" said Todd Ettleman, Van Meter's vice president of sales for its central business unit. "That really stuck with me. It's a beacon. It's like a 'we're open' sign."

Van Meter staff never knew what they would find when they inspected businesses. Heavy machinery had been unbolted and carried several feet. Deer were found walking around on the second floor of one factory. In some cases, furniture, equipment and electrical systems were a complete loss.

"Flooding is a disaster in itself. Flooding, when you add current, is a whole different level of devastation – complexity, damage, risk," Ettleman said.

The demand for replacement electrical systems and equipment for flooded busi-

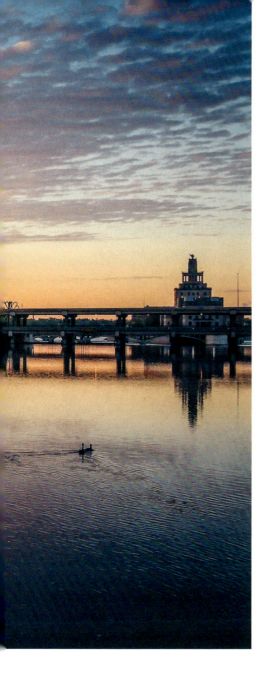

nesses was nonstop for weeks. Employees from Van Meter's other 12 branches across the state, as well as locations in Minnesota, came to Cedar Rapids to fill orders in the warehouse. They worked more hours and a second shift was added to tackle the influx of shipping orders. Additional drivers were hired to deliver equipment to customers.

"We had to add extra shifts because so much inventory was coming in and it was going off the shelves just as fast," recalled Justin Haller, a Van Meter account specialist, who took additional shifts, not only because he wanted to help, but because he had a new baby at home and his wife's business downtown had flooded.

At the same time, several employees' homes were also flooded. The company and coworkers helped with the cleanup and recovery of those houses, as well. The round-the-clock work, along with the experience of the flood, took an emotional toll on Van Meter staff. To cope, the company and employees donated time, money and equipment to businesses and the community totaling $750,000. Van Meter adopted several flooded businesses to help them recover.

"We didn't feel good about making a profit from the flood. So, we decided to take 20 percent above our net goal and give it back to the community," Gassmann said. "And adoption for us didn't mean just giving money. It meant ripping out drywall, ripping out carpet, helping them rebuild as much as we possibly could. We helped them clean up and then we donated product to get them back up and running. The flood was one of the saddest moments and one of the proudest moments of our company and it hit us all really hard."

Lura McBride, Van Meter's president and CEO, said the flood and subsequent recovery has been a defining moment for Cedar Rapids, which is a source of pride and humility for the employee-owned company.

"My drive to work takes me through the Kingston area and I can remember how dark it was; every home was devastated," she said. "And I can remember the very first house that had their lights on, the very first family back in the neighborhood. Then slowly but surely, as I drove down that street, a couple weeks later, there were a few more on. One by one, lights would come on and you would see the people coming back in. It's a really vibrant neighborhood again."

Manufacturer reels, recovers from flooding

One of the many businesses Van Meter employees toured after the flood was Diamond V, a global producer of animal nutrition products serving 75 countries. Diamond V's headquarters and production facility, located across the river from Quaker Oats, were filled with water.

Before the flood, Diamond V officials and employees were keeping a careful eye on the rising waters but weren't expecting it to flood. Weather experts predicted the river would crest at 24 feet, and the city protected itself to 26 feet, but the river rose to 31.12 feet.

"We were caught a little bit off guard because we thought it was going to be less urgent than it ended up being," said Jeff Cannon, Diamond V's president and CEO. "When we received our evacuation orders, we were really scrambling to get product out of our plant and equipment in our main office moved."

The company was unable to remove most of its inventory from the facility before the flood.

"Interstate 380 was like a parking lot and our trucks couldn't get through the traffic," he said. "So, we ended up losing a significant amount of inventory that we had on the floor."

The next day, company employees met at Kirkwood Community College's convention center.

"Our CEO and President John Bloomhall assured everyone that they wouldn't lose their jobs, that Diamond V would survive; they didn't have to worry about their paychecks, they were going to continue getting paid, no matter how long we were down," Cannon said. "And if they had their own personal situation with the flood, they needed to go home and take care of it and let us know what they needed so we could help them."

The operations, manufacturing and procurement teams began working on an action plan for what to do after they regained access to the company's only factory.

"We flew a plane over our manufacturing plant and took pictures to see how high the water was so we could get a better understanding of what sort of water we were going to have inside the facility when the river crested," Cannon said.

While the plant was flooding, Diamond V reached out to vendors, electrical contractors, plumbers and other contractors needed to restore the facility. Many of them had worked with the facility for years and knew what part to order to make it operational. About five days after the crest, Diamond V was allowed to return to its facilities.

"We hit the ground running," Cannon said.

The company and city of Cedar Rapids worked together to ensure Diamond V had the power, gas, water and sewer systems needed to function.

"Everything we needed, they were able to get it for us so we could get the plant up and running again," Cannon said.

A disaster recovery company was contracted to bring in generators and other equipment and clean the facility. Diamond V was the first manufacturer in Cedar Rapids to open after the flood passed.

"We scrubbed the place from foot to toe and had contractors in there replacing all the motors, electrical systems, control boxes – everything needed to get back up and

"WE DIDN'T ASK FOR A CLEAN SHEET OF PAPER, BUT WE GOT ONE AND WE'RE MAKING IT BETTER. WE CAN SEE A BRIGHT FUTURE AND WE KNOW WE CAN TRIUMPH OVER ADVERSITY," SAID JEFF CANNON, PRESIDENT AND CEO OF DIAMOND V IN CEDAR RAPIDS.

Opposite, top and bottom: *Diamond V facility and office flooding (Diamond V).*

Left: *Employees clean factory equipment after the flood (Diamond V).*

running," he said. "On the evening of July 4, we had the equipment back up and we started our first run, our first product off the processing line. We were the very first flood-affected manufacturer in that flood zone to come back online. [The cleanup and recovery] was literally 24/7."

Every night, Bloomhall sent an email to Diamond V teams in Canada, Mexico, Netherlands, China, Thailand and other countries to keep them updated on recovery progress and inventory levels.

"They helped us move product around so we could get product where it was needed and our customers helped us make sure that product was being allocated to the right places," Cannon said. "As a result of that, none of our customers ran out of product."

Bloomhall, who has since retired, was named one of four finalists in the Ernst & Young Entrepreneur of the Year competition in 2010, in part because of the company's ability to bounce back.

The award was one of many company milestones since the flood.

In 2009, Diamond V finished construction of a new $26 million facility. In 2012, the company completed a $4.5 million headquarters and $12.5 million factory expansion. Diamond V celebrated its 75th anniversary in 2017 and announced its acquisition by Cargill, which will allow Diamond V to expand into more countries. In 2018, the company will complete a $28 million expansion in Cedar Rapids.

"As we look back on it, the flood was one of those events that really re-energized us and re-committed us to our team and our organization. It was a struggle, but a lot of good things came out of that event," Cannon said. "We really saw our business accelerate after 2008. We got more innovative, we took more risks; we didn't retreat into a shell."

The renewed focus on innovation led to a major breakthrough. Diamond V made a significant investment in research and development and from that, the company developed products that reduce antibiotic resistance and lower foodborne pathogens in animals.

"We're making discoveries that we really feel a huge social responsibility to bring to the marketplace," Cannon said.

Distributing sandbags and pouring concrete

During the days before the flood, King's Material was a busy place. Trucks lined up to the company entrance to load up on sandbags. The company gave away and sold more than 200,000 for flood protection. These days, the company keeps 250,000 sandbags on reserve in case the river surprises Cedar Rapids again.

King's Material, a ready-mix concrete manufacturer, has been in business since 1882. When the 2008 flood crested, the company's 12th Avenue office filled with water, despite its location several blocks west of the Cedar River.

"We had water up to the second desk drawers in the office and even more in the warehouse," President Charlie Rohde said.

King's Material is owned by Rohde's family's company, Dakota Red Corp., which also operates Midland Concrete Products and Hawkeye Ready-Mix, with locations in Cedar Rapids, Coralville, Marshalltown and Waterloo.

During the flood, the company's Waterloo, Coralville and 12th Avenue Cedar Rapids locations took on water, causing $350,000 in damage. At the 12th Avenue office, the phone system, heating and cooling ducts and furniture were wiped out. Company vehicles were flooded and concrete block was submerged.

"We had a lot of ruined inventory," Rohde recalled. "But we were so much better off than a lot of people."

Employees and operations were moved to the company's 50th Avenue Drive

Opposite: Top, Diamond V hung a banner to thank the many vendors and contractors who helped the company become operational again. Bottom, former Diamond V CEO and President John Bloomhall thanks employees and vendors during a flood recovery celebration. Right, Diamond V's new corporate headquarters (Diamond V).

Top: *Water creeps into King's Material's 12 Avenue facility in Cedar Rapids.*

Above: *King's Material's President Charlie Rohde wades through flooding (King's Material).*

Above: *King's Material's 12th Avenue facility today, top; the same building during the flood, bottom (King's Material).*

Opposite: *King's Material's 50th Avenue Drive location (King's Material).*

location where offices were shared and folding tables and chairs were set up in the hallways and lobby for the various teams.

"It was kind of fun for a while but I wouldn't want to do it forever," Rohde said. "But with our multiple facilities and resources, we were able to recover quite quickly."

During that time, the company was attending to its employees and retirees who were affected by the flood.

"You just couldn't go anywhere without your friends being impacted," he said. "You couldn't help but feel so bad for all the people in Time Check and the Czech Village losing their homes."

On the bright side, the flood allowed those historic neighborhoods to receive much needed updates.

"I go through the Czech Village every day going to and from work," he said. "All those little worker houses were built back in the early 1900s, many of which are very well maintained. But if you looked at a lot of them [pre-flood], they needed a new roof or a new electrical system, it's probably the original sewer and water pipes. Had there not been the tragedy, there probably wasn't going to be anybody to step up and say, 'we need to renovate 2,500 houses.' It's a shame to lose a lot of those old neighborhoods, but parts of those neighborhoods did need to be renovated. You can see the pride is still right there. The flood did a favor for a lot of parts of town."

After the flood, when the city was down to one well for drinking water, King's Material stopped producing concrete to help save water. The company sold undamaged-yet-flooded concrete block at a discount to help rebuild foundations and basements. Company dump trucks were loaned out to businesses needing to haul debris. The company poured cement block for the basement of the U.S. Bank building downtown and repaired countless streets and buildings where small chunks of concrete had washed away.

The company contracted on work for several flood recovery projects in Cedar Rapids, including the U.S. federal courthouse, civic center and CRST tower and parking projects. Since then, the company has experienced continued growth and has

unveiled new product lines.

"In 2008, recovery was important," Rohde said. "The recession had just started. I think the flood actually kind of helped us for a few years. Normally, if we're in a recession, the construction market dries up. We had a number of projects there for a few years that kept us, not totally normal, but better than what they would have been. We've stayed busy, we've kept all our people working, which is important to us."

In 2016, when water rose to dangerously high levels again, King's Material jumped into action.

"We had trucks out until 11 p.m. Sunday night and we were making a lot of concrete," Rohde said.

Back in 2008, water had filled storm and sewer pipes, drained, and then returned through the pipes again, compounding the flood damage.

"Downtown, you'd pump out a basement and then come back the next day and it would be full of water," he said. "The water was just going back and forth between the buildings."

So, in 2016, King's Material filled pipes with concrete to stem the flooding.

"We were clogging pipes. There's an 8-foot diameter pipe down by Eighth Avenue and we dumped 100 yards of concrete down it to keep the river from coming back and flooding Mercy hospital," Rohde said.

The method worked and did much to reduce flooding in 2016 but is not viewed as a long-term flood prevention measure. Public officials and business leaders are acutely aware that more flood protection is needed. Despite the wait for some projects, several flood prevention measures have been installed since 2008.

"We've got these new buildings downtown, like the new CRST building," Rohde said. "To the public, that's a block of a free floodwall. The [McGrath] Amphitheatre, that's a floodwall. There have been a lot of creative pieces coming into this that are going to help like crazy. 2016 (flooding) showed we still have a lot of work to do in terms of protecting ourselves. But if we're going to do it, let's do it right and let's prepare for it being a little higher next time."

"I'M PROUD OF OUR CITY. I'M PROUD OF THE PEOPLE," SAID CHARLIE ROHDE, PRESIDENT OF KING'S MATERIAL AND CEO OF DAKOTA RED CORP., WHO SERVES AS CHAIRMAN OF THE CEDAR RAPIDS METRO ECONOMIC ALLIANCE.

Mucking out 1,126 city blocks

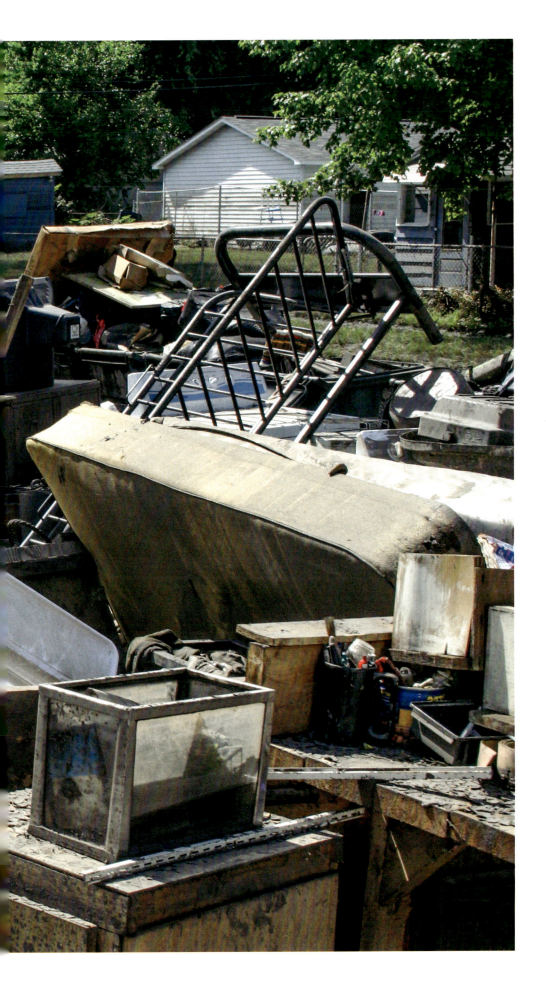

After the waters receded, the massive task of cleaning out homes and businesses began in mid-June. Neighbors helped neighbors empty homes of debris and employees teamed up to do the same at flooded businesses.

Contractors and city staff assessed damage at each structure before they could be reinhabited. Some homes and businesses were a complete loss. For most, all furniture and many keepsakes needed to be thrown away. More than 42,000 tons of debris was removed from 1,126 flood-affected city blocks. Cleanup was delayed at some buildings as asbestos testing and abatement was completed.

There were many health concerns, including mold exposure, contaminated water and potential injuries from wading through flood debris. Several mobile clinics were set up to administer tetanus shots. Residents were advised to wear face masks and gloves.

Once furniture and other debris were removed and damage assessed, the power washing and disinfecting began. The river water had left a foul-smelling, slick-yet-sticky mud on everything it touched.

Hundreds of cleanup crews and

Flood-damaged household items, furniture and heirlooms sit curbside awaiting garbage pick up (Alliant Energy).

"I CAN'T STRESS ENOUGH THE GOODNESS OF THE PEOPLE WHO CAME WITHOUT INVITATION," SAID JACK EVANS, PRESIDENT, HALL-PERRINE FOUNDATION. "THAT WAS REALLY PROFOUND TO ME."

Above, top and bottom: *Workers in masks and jumpsuits empty out a flooded building, top (City of Cedar Rapids); once flood waters receded, thousands of homes were cleaned out and disinfected, bottom (Alliant Energy).*

Opposite: *Volunteers make repairs to flood-damaged homes, above, and the Greater Cedar Rapids Community Foundation office (Greater Cedar Rapids Community Foundation).*

volunteers came from across the country to help. Some were from national disaster recovery companies, others were from church groups and some came on their own to "muck out" homes and businesses.

"I can't stress enough the goodness of the people who came without invitation," said Jack Evans, president of the Hall-Perrine Foundation. "That was really profound to me."

Nonprofit community partnerships provide relief

The Greater Cedar Rapids Community Foundation (GCRCF) partnered with dozens of area nonprofits to provide help and relief to flooded residents and businesses. More than $5.7 million was given by 2,200 donors from 43 states and four countries to the Flood 2008 Fund. Roughly $15 million was raised for local nonprofits through the fund, business donations and other gifts.

During the first days and weeks after the flood, nonprofits and business groups visited with residents and business owners to hear their needs. Those surveys resulted in immediate infusions of cash. Within three months, the foundation had distributed $290,000 from its operating reserves to help more than 60 nonprofits get back to business.

By the end of the year, millions of dollars in grants and other donations were distributed to help with household essentials, cleanup costs and business losses. GCRCF grants of $5,000 each were provided to local nonprofits to help them remain operational during flood cleanup and recovery. Additional grants focused on long-term needs of the community, such as affordable housing, emotional trauma services and

"THERE'S AN INTANGIBLE SENSE OF COMMUNITY AND COHESION THAT RESULTED FROM THE FLOOD. IT HELPED THE ENTIRE COMMUNITY DEFINE WHO WE ARE AND CREATED THIS SPIRIT OF VOLUNTEERISM," SAID KARLA TWEDT-BALL, SENIOR VICE PRESIDENT, PROGRAMS AND COMMUNITY INVESTMENT AT GREATER CEDAR RAPIDS COMMUNITY FOUNDATION.

other systematic needs.

Perhaps the most significant program was Block by Block, a partnership between Matthew 25 Ministry Hub, Four Oaks' Affordable Housing Network and the United Methodist Church. The groups worked together to help families in the worst-hit neighborhoods west of the river. They focused on one block at a time and utilized the large influx of volunteers from outside Cedar Rapids. Volunteers repaired homes, by fixing damaged foundations, among other improvements.

The program started with a grant of $1.2 million from GCRCF and $1 million from CRST International Chairman and Owner John Smith and his wife, Dyan. Overall, more than $4.6 million was spent on 25 blocks, renovating more than 250 homes.

"You can't help a child unless you help the family and you can't help the family unless you help the neighborhood," said Les Garner, GCRCF's president and CEO. "The flood affected core neighborhoods and this work helped to focus the attention on those issues and neighborhoods."

Flood Them with Love was a grassroots initiative started by Karla Goettel, whose goal was to help one family who lost everything in the flood. She encouraged a few

friends to participate and before long, it became a community-wide program that raised $500,000 for more than 350 families.

"What amazed me over and over again was all the ways people stepped up to be helpful," said Karla Twedt-Ball, senior vice president of programs and community investment at GCRCF. "It was such a community effort. I think it reinforced in the community our can-do attitude and hospitality."

Iowa Legal Aid developed a program to help flooded homeowners with the paperwork necessary to receive buyouts and other assistance. Horizons, A Family Service Alliance provided credit counseling to those experiencing financial hardships.

Since that time, GCRCF has grown considerably in staff size and donations.

"The flood helped increase our visibility in the community as a catalyst, as a problem solver and as a source of thoughtful grant-making," Garner said.

The flood fund grants helped residents and businesses not only recover from the flood, but heal, as well, Twedt-Ball said.

"There's an intangible sense of community and cohesion that resulted from the flood. It helped the entire community define who we are and created this spirit of volunteerism," she said. "With the flood, it was a shared experience, a group grief, and it was overwhelming, but we were all going through it together and we were able to make it."

Many other organizations and donors also contributed to recovery efforts. United Way of East Central Iowa and its partners, including Four Oaks, HACAP, The Arc and Waypoint, were on the frontlines from the beginning, capitalizing on community partnerships to make sure residents received help. Businesses, nonprofits and foundations raised and distributed millions of dollars for residents and recovery. For example, the Hall-Perrine Foundation provided $25 million in grants to several of the same agencies.

Opposite and above: *Thousands of volunteers worked to clean and repair homes in Cedar Rapids as part of the Block by Block Program (Greater Cedar Rapids Community Foundation).*

First-of-its-kind business recovery program

Federal, state and local entities partnered with business groups to create a variety of business recovery funding programs after the flood. One such program was the first of its kind in the country.

"JumpStart2 Business, and the predecessor program JumpStart, represent perhaps one of the most successful public/private partnerships in the history of our city, and perhaps a model for the nation," said Capstone Charity Resources founder Theresa Bornbach, who served as the business support strategist at the Cedar Rapids Metro Economic Alliance from 2014 to 2016. "Before the flood waters began to recede, a small band of local business owners began meeting to determine what would need to be done to begin and sustain the recovery of small business in the flood ravaged area of Cedar Rapids."

Opposite: *Little Bohemia in the New Bohemia District proudly displays its open flag (Angela Holmes).*

Above: *Czech Village mainstay Sykora Bakery has fully recovered and welcomes new and longtime patrons (Cindy Hadish).*

Above: *Signs and banners were common during and after the flood in Cedar Rapids (Alliant Energy, Corridor Business Journal, City of Cedar Rapids).*

Opposite: *Brewhemia in the New Bohemia District is one of the many post-flood business success stories (William P. Buckets).*

The U.S. Department of Housing and Urban Development, Iowa Economic Development Authority, Rebuild Iowa Office, East Central Iowa Council of Governments, City of Cedar Rapids, Cedar Rapids Metro Area Economic Alliance and other groups joined to create the Cedar Rapids Small Business Recovery Group. The U.S. Small Business Administration, SCORE and Small Business Development Center also lent support.

"The partners worked together to establish the first-of-its-kind forgivable loan disaster recovery program for businesses impacted by the disaster," Bornbach said. "In the past, loans were provided by the SBA and others to businesses that sustained damage in natural disasters. But Iowa recovery would be hampered by loans, some bearing interest, to areas with such significant impacts to small businesses."

Funding came initially from local businesses and the city of Cedar Rapids, followed by state investments. The first checks were distributed by October 2008.

"The benefit of this early funding, approximately $13 million, was that it was state [economic development] funding, which allowed significant flexibility in the definition of the program," Bornbach said. "However, by late fall, due to the concentrated losses in Cedar Rapids, the decision was made to move the funding mechanism to federal HUD (Housing and Urban Development) and CDBG (Community Development Block Grant) funding."

The Job and Small Business Recovery Fund provided $6 million in forgivable loan grants, while Jump Start added $19 million, and $1.7 million came from national emergency grant funding through Kirkwood Community College. But it wasn't enough to cover business losses in Cedar Rapids.

Business leaders created JumpStart2, an improved business recovery program, which ended up providing $85 million.

"Everyone knew that a flood-impacted business could never be made whole, but we knew we had to give them a start," Bornbach said. "While this effort was perhaps one of the most comprehensive partnerships to date in supporting disaster recovery, it was not without controversy and contentious discussion. There simply wasn't

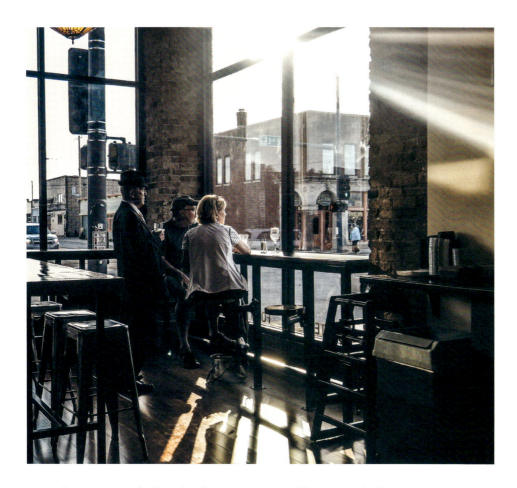

"HISTORY TOLD US WE WOULD LOSE MORE THAN 50 PERCENT OF THE BUSINESSES IMPACTED BY THE DISASTER. AT THE END OF THE PROGRAM, LESS THAN 20 PERCENT OF BUSINESS WERE NO LONGER OPERATING," SAID THERESA BORNBACH, FOUNDER, CAPSTONE CHARITY RESOURCES.

enough money. And when funds are scarce, and losses are high, discussion can be difficult."

Eight business initiatives were created with the funding, including business rental assistance, inventory and equipment replacement, loan interest reimbursement, commercial rent gap, residential landlord assistance and flood insurance reimbursement programs.

These programs helped businesses when insurance and basic federal programs didn't. For example, traditional reimbursement programs didn't reimburse for fixtures, some equipment and other building needs. Additionally, recovery needed to be swift. To receive federal disaster assistance, however, much documentation is required. Businesses often didn't have the time or resources to fill in the piles of paperwork, so the partnership helped reduce those barriers to funding.

More than 1,200 businesses applied for these funding programs. Many Cedar Rapids non-flooded companies participated in an adopt-a-business program by helping flooded businesses clean up and recover from the flood. Assistance included providing temporary facilities, business coaching, financial assistance and more.

Cedar Rapids was able to beat the odds when it came to post-flood business recovery, in large part because of these programs. Typically, half of disaster-affected businesses permanently close after an event like the 2008 Midwestern U.S. Floods.

"At the end of the program, less than 20 percent of businesses were no longer operating. And remember, this was in the middle of the most significant economic downturn in decades," Bornbach said. "The relationships built and those that had to be rebuilt stood the test of time and our business community is stronger than ever."

Corridor Rising

Kirkwood becomes a business, government hub

"AFTER THE FLOOD, THE RECESSION CAME AND WE WENT FROM 15,000 TO 19,000 STUDENTS IN ENROLLMENT IN A TWO-YEAR PERIOD. A LOT OF PEOPLE WERE HURTING AND A LOT PEOPLE REACHED OUT TO KIRKWOOD FOR THAT NEXT STEP, TO GET THEMSELVES RIGHTED, TO GET THEMSELVES BACK ON TRACK, TO GET THE SKILLS TRAINING THEY NEEDED," SAID MICK STARCEVICH, THEN PRESIDENT, KIRKWOOD COMMUNITY COLLEGE.

Kirkwood Community College opened its doors to several government agencies and businesses evacuated from neighborhoods near the river. The college's 680-acre site became a business hub because of its meeting space, available technology and location — near downtown, but far from the river. The Kirkwood Center for Continuing Education was also the site of daily press conferences on the flood.

Kirkwood's emergency management response center hosted federal marshals, U.S. Immigrations and Customs, Federal Emergency Management Agency (FEMA), Homeland Security, state and county agencies, as well as city of Cedar Rapids departments such as police, fire, housing, mayor and city council. Because most of Linn County's facilities were flooded, the county's courthouse and other services were also moved to Kirkwood.

"The center is high technology, so there's screens all around to see what's happening and help make decisions with disaster planning," said Mick Starcevich, Kirkwood Community College's then-president.

The campus also became a temporary home for 1,200 animals evacuated from homes, farms and animal shelters. Kirkwood later offered the city free land to rebuild

Right: *Kirkwood Community College hosted then-President George W. Bush, where he was briefed by Federal Emergency Management Agency officials (U.S. Government Publishing Office).*

Opposite, top and bottom: *Emergency management personnel gather at Kirkwood Community College to coordinate flood preparation, rescue and recovery efforts (Kirkwood Community College).*

CEDAR RIVER

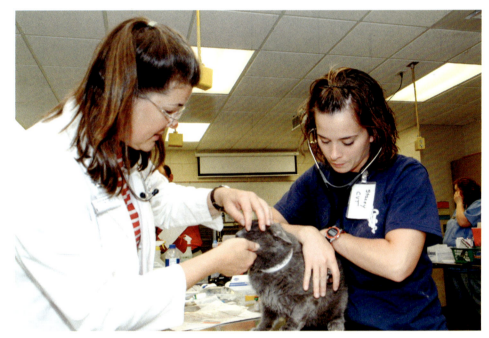

More than 1,200 animals called Kirkwood Community College home during the flood, as residents were forced to evacuate the area. Kirkwood students and community volunteers cared for the animals. As a result, Kirkwood developed the Midwest's only animal humane officer training program. (Kirkwood Community College).

Opposite: When NewBo City Market was built in 2012, Kirkwood added a culinary center to the market to increase student training (Kirkwood Community College).

its animal control services. "In exchange for the land, they built us a classroom so the students could go over and get experience in animal control," Starcevich said.

As a result, Kirkwood developed the Midwest's only animal humane officer training program. Later, when NewBo City Market was built near downtown in 2012, Kirkwood added a culinary center there to increase student training.

"Because of all this engagement and cross-communication among many different entities – education, city government, emergency management and businesses that needed assistance, it has really helped with our partnership and communication," said Kim Becicka, vice president of continuing education and training services with Kirkwood Community College. "And great facilities have come from that, especially for the arts and culture community."

Seventeen businesses set up shop at Kirkwood in 2008, including AEGON, Alliant Energy, Diamond V, GCRCF and more. Kirkwood's Small Business Development Center was also heavily involved with post-flood business recovery, helping business owners with paperwork for disaster assistance. Kirkwood also tapped into federal funding for displaced workers to pay them wages for flood recovery work.

"The [post-flood] investment that's been made, in addition to the collaborations, have positioned the region's quality of life in a way that continues to grow our population, which we need to have to meet our workforce development demands of our growing employer base. And we're way ahead of where we would have been before the flood, because of the new downtown housing and amenities," Becicka said.

Enrollment increased at the college during that time, as the national recession worsened.

"After the flood, the recession came and we went from 15,000 to 19,000 students in enrollment in a two-year period. A lot of people were hurting and a lot people reached out to Kirkwood for that next step, to get themselves righted, to get themselves back on track, to get the skills training they needed. Now look at it, we have the lowest unemployment rate in history," Starcevich said.

Home buyouts, flood mitigation plans begin

With cleanup well underway, Cedar Rapids turned its attention to the $6 billion in damage the city experienced. Officials began the lengthy discussions and plans of restoring services and rebuilding facilities. More than 300 city buildings were flooded, so many of the city's most vital services were relocated. Officials started to create short- and long-term plans for future flood mitigation, and began rehabilitation and replacement of damaged city buildings, residential neighborhoods, business districts and arts and cultural landmarks. City leaders met twice daily with residents and business leaders to determine the greatest immediate needs and create priorities for ongoing recovery.

To ensure basic needs were met, plans were created for 10 residential neighborhoods to review flood zones and discuss home buyouts. Overall, 4,766 homes were damaged and inspected by city officials. Local, state and federal funds provided $147.3 million to acquire and demolish 1,375 flooded houses. Homes were razed to prevent future risk to residents and to create pathways for future flooding and reduce potential storm damage.

The University of Iowa Flood Center, created in 2009, utilizes research and expertise from the UI's hydrology department to monitor waterways and help prevent future flooding losses. The center developed flood models to help Cedar Rapids assess future flooding risk to various properties.

FEMA's Hazard Mitigation Grant Program (HMGP) and the U.S. Department of Housing and Urban Development's Community Development Block Grant Program

Right: *Many residents stayed in trailers provided by the Federal Emergency Management Agency after the flood (City of Cedar Rapids).*

Opposite: *Linn County Command Center (United Way).*

(CDBG) provided important funding for buyouts, which were complete after five years. State funding came largely from the I-JOBS initiative, created to boost state economic development and fund flood recovery projects.

When business leaders traveled to Grand Forks, North Dakota, shortly after the 2008 flood to seek advice from various officials there who had experienced a severe flood in 1997, they were warned to expect leadership turnover in every industry sector, including city government. That's exactly what happened. Former Mayor Kay Halloran did not seek re-election in 2009 and was succeeded by Ron Corbett. Former City Manager Jim Prosser retired from his position in 2010 and was replaced by Jeff Pomeranz, who had served in the same position in West Des Moines.

The flood response, cleanup and immediate recovery was exhausting work. Several local business leaders have said Corbett, Pomeranz and city staff brought a fresh energy and enthusiasm to the flood recovery.

"I was city manager in West Des Moines at the time of the flooding in 2008," Pomeranz said. "After the flood, I was appointed by the governor to chair the I-JOBS board, an entity with the responsibility to distribute close to $2 million to flood-impacted communities. We quickly identified needs across the state, including in Cedar Rapids and the Eastern Iowa Corridor. I was impressed with the leadership in Cedar Rapids, including the city, county and the business sector. There became a city manager opening in Cedar Rapids, and because of how impressed I was with work happening in the city, I eventually was offered and accepted the position."

City staff and leaders had spent the first two years after the flood applying for and negotiating with state and federal entities to secure funding assistance for projects. Housing buyout money began to arrive in 2010 and city staff quickly began to act on several projects.

"WHEN PEOPLE RETURNED, THEY DIDN'T WORRY ABOUT PETTY THINGS, THEY WERE JUST HAPPY TO BE BACK," SAID CHEYRL HINES, ADMINISTRATOR, SIMMONS PERRINE MOYER BERGMAN PLC IN CEDAR RAPIDS.

Putting future flood protection into place

Many leaders in Cedar Rapids agree that while several flood protection systems have been installed since the 2008 flood, more are needed. The city of Cedar Rapids has completed a handful of flood protection projects and is in the process of constructing more, as part of its long-term flood mitigation plan. The $400 million-plus in improvements are paid for with a combination of local, state and federal grants and loans.

"Knowing permanent flood protection would take many years to complete, our staff updated our interim flood protection plan," Pomeranz said. "Many improvements were put in place, based on new knowledge acquired from battling flooding in 2008. This improved planning was put to the test in September 2016 when our city was once again facing record flooding. Thankfully, our planning efforts paid off and we were able to fight off what could have potentially been another devastating event."

Since 2008, businesses and government organizations have constructed new buildings in downtown Cedar Rapids with flood protection features. They added flood walls, improved sewer systems, elevated water infrastructure and moved utilities, among other enhancements. Home buyouts removed more than 1,300 properties from the flood zone and made way for additional greenspace along the river to provide more of a flood buffer between the waterway and downtown. Two bridges over Prairie Creek were raised to reduce debris bottlenecks during future high waters. The CRST Center office tower includes a floodwall, gatewell and pump station.

The McGrath Amphitheatre was completed in 2014 for $8 million on the river's

Above: *The McGrath Amphitheatre in Kingston Village doubles as a floodwall (John Richard).*

Opposite, top: *Sandbag walls in the New Bohemia District (Corridor Business Journal).*

Opposite, bottom: *Rendering of Sinclair Levee and Gates (City of Cedar Rapids).*

west side. The venue has hosted a number of popular artists, such as Nelly and Diana Ross. The facility is floodable and serves as a flood levee when necessary.

The $15-million Sinclair levee, which protects to 2008 flood levels, is equipped with a trail for pedestrians and bicyclists.

Soon to be completed are:
• A 4.4-acre detention basin providing flood protection during heavy rain events and can dramatically reduce the storm water runoff rate.
• The Lot 44 Pump Station, able to pump 12,000 gallons per minute and includes gates to protect against water backing up through storm sewers.
• The half-mile-long Czech Village levee, which will protect to the 2008 water level.

The city of Cedar Rapids continues to enact additional flood protection plans and install flood mitigation projects such as more floodwalls and levees, replacement of the Eighth Street Bridge, construction of additional pump stations and development of more park land to absorb high water levels.

Some of these new systems and plans were put to the test in 2016, when the river reached a crest of 21.97 feet in Cedar Rapids – the city's second worst on record. Residents sandbagged and removable barriers were erected. Many watched drone coverage of the flooding, to stay abreast of where water was rising. Fortunately, damage was minimal.

After the 2008 flood, the city reorganized its communications employees. By 2016, they were all working under one manager, improving the relay of information to media, residents and businesses.

"Not only was the city better prepared to protect the community from flooding in 2016, we have also received very positive feedback regarding communication throughout the event," Pomeranz said. "We hosted daily news conferences, including a sign language interpreter and streamed using Facebook Live, provided real-time updates on our website and social media pages, regularly met with local media to provide interviews and updates, and even posted information on billboards, thanks to advertising space donated by local media companies."

"LOOKING BACK, WE WERE FORTUNATE TO HAVE LEADERS WHOSE OVERARCHING GOAL WAS TO WORK TOGETHER TO MAKE THINGS BETTER. PEOPLE TALKED AND COMMUNICATED, EVERYBODY WORKED TOGETHER," SAID TOM ALLER, FORMER ALLIANT ENERGY EXECUTIVE.

Cedar Rapids Central Business District, downtown reinvestment

"FOR US, I THINK IT WAS REALLY IMPORTANT TO DEVELOP PARTNERSHIPS TO REBUILD. THE DISASTER WAS SO MASSIVE THAT ONE ENTITY ALONE DIDN'T HAVE BROAD ENOUGH SHOULDERS TO CARRY EVERYONE," SAID RON CORBETT, FORMER MAYOR, CITY OF CEDAR RAPIDS.

In 2008, not only was downtown submerged, life as people knew it in Cedar Rapids became completely upended.

"I looked out and about (at the flood damage) and I was absolutely astounded at the water. I mean, you just can't conceive of it – that flooding, for all the years I lived here – could have such a major impact," said John Smith, CRST's chairman of the board. "We realized immediately that the businesses downtown were going to be dramatically affected, as well as the near neighborhoods."

When a flood of that magnitude hits, people tend to react with astonishment, along with a momentary paralysis as they take in the event, its damage and the aftermath. In Cedar Rapids, it was as if the city had the wind knocked out of it.

Residents and businesses, however, did not stay breathless for long. Shock turned into action. Evacuees returned. Despair transitioned into cleanup. Slowly, rebuilding became recovery and, in the process, the city recreated itself.

"We didn't ask for a clean sheet of paper, but we got one and we're making it better. We can see a bright future and we know we can triumph over adversity. The flood tested our mettle and we won. The whole Corridor is really teed up to be a mecca of growth and prosperity," said Diamond V's Jeff Cannon.

Just as they had sandbagged together, the people of Cedar Rapids rebuilt together, side by side, hand in hand.

"What a source of pride it is to walk downtown, to see NewBo and what life there is, and the way the McGrath Amphitheatre came up on the river," said Van Meter Inc.'s Lura McBride. "I greatly admire how we, as a city, decided we cannot be scared of the river, to instead celebrate the river and build around it. It took a lot of courage to not be afraid, to embrace the river. It took a lot of guts to make that happen."

Opposite: *Flooding in downtown Cedar Rapids (Alliant Energy).*

Top to bottom: *Smulekoff's furniture store, a downtown landmark since 1889, was flooded and renovated. It no longer serves as a furniture store, but as an events and multiuse space (top, Alliant Energy; middle and bottom, Corridor Business Journal).*

City, businesses partner to rebuild downtown

City staff immediately began to assess damage at its 130 flooded facilities. Owners of flooded businesses met with city leaders and staff about finding ways to renovate or relocate. Local business leaders discussed strategies for rebuilding the downtown district. Those talks set the stage for public/private partnerships that resulted in the city's major recovery projects.

"For us, I think it was really important to develop partnerships to rebuild. The disaster was so massive that one entity alone didn't have broad enough shoulders to carry everyone," said Ron Corbett, who served as mayor of Cedar Rapids from 2010 to 2018.

An important aspect of those partnerships was the commitment by the city to renovate and replace its flooded buildings. Simultaneously, business leaders vowed to reinvest in downtown.

"People look at government in times of disaster to really step up and help forge the path," Corbett said. "It was really important as a city to rebuild our own facilities. If you're not willing to invest in yourself, why would you expect others to invest in you? The community saw us invest in city hall, the library, convention center, Paramount Theatre and so on, and that gave the private sector confidence. And the public investment pales in comparison to the overall investment by the private sector."

The list of projects was at times overwhelming and many experienced sticker shock as costs added up. To make the recovery more manageable, the city broke it down into smaller chunks – one bridge, one block, one levee.

"One by one, we put the resources together," Corbett said. "When we received a grant for $35 million for the convention center, that relieved a lot of pressure."

The city applied for every grant possible to help pay for the projects, as local charitable organizations and foundations partnered to assist with funding.

The countless relationships that formed during flood evacuations and cleanup played an important part in Cedar Rapids' successful recovery.

"For us in Cedar Rapids, working to rebuild after the flood helped us build relationships and work together with local leaders throughout the region," Pomeranz said. "We were able to support each other and identify and share community resources. These relationships continue as we move past recovery and toward positioning our region for long-term success."

Cedar Rapids Downtown Farmers' Market (Cindy Hadish).

City commits to rebuild infrastructure, downtown assets

Within the first few years after the flood, several major recovery projects came online, including:

The Cedar Rapids U.S. Courthouse, Iowa's northern district federal courthouse, received awards for its design and flood protection after it was rebuilt along the Cedar River. The city assisted with the project, which had been awaiting a new building for more than 20 years. The 306,000-square-foot structure includes five courtrooms, and a law library. Nineteen government agencies are housed at the building. With LEED gold certification, the facility includes solar panels, rain water collection system and a green roof. After opening, it received design awards from the U.S. General Services Administration and Justice Facilities Review. Cost: $182 million.

"For the community there were definitely a lot of positives that came from the flood," said Larry Helling, president and CEO of Cedar Rapids Bank and Trust. "If it

Below: *The Cedar Rapids U.S. Courthouse was rebuilt along the Cedar River for $182 million (Corridor Business Journal).*

Opposite: *The 275-room DoubleTree by Hilton Hotel anchors downtown activity (Miranda Meyer).*

"THE (POST-FLOOD) INVESTMENT THAT'S BEEN MADE, IN ADDITION TO THE COLLABORATIONS, HAVE POSITIONED THE REGION'S QUALITY OF LIFE IN A WAY THAT CONTINUES TO GROW OUR POPULATION, WHICH WE NEED TO MEET OUR WORKFORCE DEVELOPMENT DEMANDS OF OUR GROWING EMPLOYER BASE" SAID KIM BECICKA, VICE PRESIDENT, CONTINUING EDUCATION AND TRAINING SERVICES, KIRKWOOD COMMUNITY COLLEGE.

weren't for the flood, we would have waited 25 years instead of five years for some of the improvements. With the federal courthouse, we were on the waiting list for a new building for years and we probably never would have made it to the top. When the flood happened, suddenly we were on the top of the list."

In 2010, the city of Cedar Rapids decided to buy the flooded and outdated Crowne Plaza Five Seasons Hotel and remodel it and the adjacent U.S. Cellular Center, a 6,900-seat events arena. The 275-room, renovated hotel is now the DoubleTree by Hilton Hotel and anchors the north end of downtown, within walking distance of dozens of corporate and small businesses, government offices, shops, restaurants and bars and event venues. On the hotel's 16th floor is 350 First, where fine cuisine is served for lunch and dinner, and for breakfast, guests can enjoy many options, including oatmeal from – and views of – the landmark Quaker Oats mill across the street.

The new 435,000-square-foot U.S. Cellular Center is the state's second largest convention and events center. It is routinely booked for business conferences, sporting and music events. The facility includes 80,000 square feet of meeting and banquet space, accommodating up to 10,000 visitors. Cost: $144 million.

"When you look at how downtown is being rejuvenated; it's amazing," Diamond V's Jeff Cannon said. "We've got visitors showing up this afternoon and they're staying at the DoubleTree downtown. We're going to take them to the new restaurants downtown for dinner. We're taking them to some events going on down there. We have a number of employees who decided they want to live downtown. It's unbelievable the transformation over the last 10 years in the flood-affected area. It's been phenomenal."

The Cedar Rapids Ground Transportation Center was repaired, renovated and expanded following the flood. Services were improved to accommodate increased safety and additional modes of transportation, including pedestrian, bicycle, wheelchair and vehicle transit. Offices, a conference room, visitor areas and enhanced restrooms were added to the building. Bus traffic flow was improved and adjacent streets were

modified to improve routes. Cost: $10.5 million.

"We were one of the contractors to work on the Ground Transportation Center," said King's Material's president Charlie Rohde. "The flood was so tragic, we were so fortunate to receive the federal funding we did to repair and improve buildings that were damaged."

Changes were made to the former City Hall building on May's Island after the flood. Veterans Memorial Building was 70 percent damaged in 2008. It has since been remodeled and the building's Grant Wood stained glass memorial window was restored. The structure now includes a military museum and several enhanced spaces for veterans' services. Cost: $18 million.

The Linn County Courthouse, also located on May's Island, was renovated. The first floor is now courtrooms, which can easily be evacuated if flood waters rise again. Cost: $8.5 million. The county jail was rebuilt for $7.6 million and the Jean Oxley Linn County Public Service Center was renovated for $14.8 million; both include extensive flood protection features.

"I know a lot of people thought, 'how could our founding fathers have ever thought in their right mind to build a city on this river and put a courthouse and city hall on an island?' After all this devastation, it's a beautiful place to live and work," said Supervisor John Harris. "When I come to work from Palo, a lot of times I'll take the boulevard along the river. The trip is a little bit longer but I get to drive along the river and it's a sight to behold. In the spring, in the summer, in the fall and even in the winter, it's a great place to live and the river makes it a better place to live."

The city of Cedar Rapids moved its offices from the Veterans Memorial Building on May's Island into the former Cedar Rapids U.S. Courthouse. The former federal courthouse became the new city hall after it was renovated and updated with flood protections and service improvements. The project received a design excellence award from AIA Chicago. Cost: $7.5 million.

"We've received a lot of positive feedback from residents who really enjoy using this building, how easy it is to get in and out and its downtown location," Corbett said.

Several arts and cultural landmarks have since been renovated, remodeled or re-

Above: *The Veterans Memorial Building was remodeled after the flood (William P. Buckets).*

Right: *The former federal courthouse was converted into the City of Cedar Rapids City Hall (Miranda Meyer).*

Opposite: *Top, the new $45 million Cedar Rapids Public Library (Knutson Construction); below, the National Czech & Slovak Museum & Library was moved and renovated after the flood (John Richard, Alliant Energy).*

located to protect against future flooding, such as:

After the federal government announced it wouldn't fund rebuilding of the Cedar Rapids Public Library in its flooded location, it moved to the former TrueNorth building, facing Greene Square Park. The information and technology hub is LEED platinum certified with a green roof that manages storm water runoff. With extensive glass panels and a 200-seat auditorium facing an urban park, the library has become a downtown focal point, with more than 600,000 visits and 1 million items circulated annually. The Cedar Rapids Public Library was one of 10 recipients of the 2017 National Medal for Museum and Library Service from the Institute of Museum and Library Services. Cost: $45 million.

"My grandson goes to a world-class public library that's always full of people," said Jack Evans, Hall-Perrine Foundation's president. "Having successful flood recovery projects like that goes a long way toward the community's healing from the flood.

The National Czech & Slovak Museum & Library (NCSML) underwent a $25 million restoration, renovation and expansion, including the move and 11-foot elevation of the building. The improved building is LEED gold certified and includes an expanded research library, larger exhibit space and galleries, a theater and underground parking. The project was paid for from several funding sources, including a $600,000 gift from the Czech Republic government. In 2017, NCSML received American Association for State and Local History's Leadership in History award for its curriculum and school tour program. The NCSML was one of 10 recipients of the Institute of Museum and Library Services' 2013 National Medal for Museum and Library Services.

The Paramount Theatre, a 1928 movie palace listed on the National Register of Historic Places, experienced $16 million in damage. Technical and aesthetic components were upgraded and the theater reopened in 2012. The restoration project was named a 2014 Public Works Project of the Year by the American Public Works Association. Cost: $35 million.

Theatre Cedar Rapids, the area's largest community theater, reopened in 2010 after its basement and sub-basement filled with 50 feet of water. More than $4 million in repairs were made to the building, including renovations to the auditorium stage and adding a black box space and studio. The theater's Rhinestone Barton theater pipe organ was refurbished as part of the renovations.

The African American Museum of Iowa, which celebrates the heritage of African Americans in Iowa with artifact collections, exhibits and research library, was the first nonprofit to return to its restored building, located in between the NewBo District and Czech Village. The building experienced $1.3 million in damage.

Cedar Rapids Museum of Art experienced flooding in its basement after city pipes backed up. Home to much of Grant Wood's artwork, less than 5 percent of the museum's 7,000-piece collection was affected by high water and humidity. Cleanup and restoration cost: $250,000.

The Cedar Rapids Helen G. Nassif YMCA's gyms, racquetball courts and locker rooms were flooded with 8 feet of water in 2008. Cleanup and recovery of the building took a few months and the center's 10,000 members were sent to satellite facilities until the building was ready to be reoccupied. Cost: $1.7 million.

CSPS (Czech-Slovak Prudential Society) Hall, dating back to 1890, is listed on the National Register of Historic Places. The building is host to Legion Arts' events in the NewBo neighborhood. Renovation included the installation of updated technology, heating and cooling systems, as well as improved studio and performance spaces. Cost: $7 million.

"Since the flood, there's been a lot of emphasis to have more businesses and things to do downtown," said Randy Ramlo, president and CEO of United Fire Group, which decided to rebuild and expand downtown after the flood. "The restaurants are full, there's a lot of activity and people really want to be downtown. That's a change from how it was before the flood. Everyone had the philosophy, 'let's build it back better than it was before.'"

Private sector rebuilds, expands downtown

During the decade after the flood, the city of Cedar Rapids provided millions of dollars in tax incentives to lure businesses downtown. The city invested in the former Five Seasons hotel, now the DoubleTree by Hilton Hotel, to help convince business leaders of the city's commitment to downtown.

"The confidence of our business community is critical to our city's long-term success," Pomeranz said. "After the flood in 2008, we worked hard to put a plan in place both for permanent flood protection and an interim plan, to show business leaders our commitment to rebuilding downtown and protecting their investments. We are very appreciative to have a large number of local businesses and developers who believe in our community and showed their long-term commitment to Cedar Rapids by investing in our downtown."

Many signs show that reinvestment and commitment has been a success.

An influx of new and renovated residential units have come online downtown since 2007. The area now has more than 670 units, a 62 percent jump from pre-flood levels.

Businesses from several industries – from banking, health care and insurance to construction, manufacturing and trucking – played an integral part in the region's recovery, ensuring continued and future growth and prosperity for the Corridor.

Since 2007, the number of businesses in town has increased 25 percent. Cedar Rapids' central downtown district today is abuzz with new and renovated small businesses from Blue Strawberry Coffee Company and Black Sheep Social Club, to White Star Ale House and Cobble Hill Eatery & Dispensary. Those businesses have set up shop amongst some of Cedar Rapids' largest and fastest growing employers.

"THE CONFIDENCE OF OUR BUSINESS COMMUNITY IS CRITICAL TO OUR CITY'S LONG-TERM SUCCESS. AFTER THE FLOOD IN 2008, WE WORKED HARD TO PUT A PLAN IN PLACE BOTH FOR PERMANENT FLOOD PROTECTION AND AN INTERIM PLAN," SAID JEFF POMERANZ, CITY MANAGER, CITY OF CEDAR RAPIDS.

Opposite: *Theatre Cedar Rapids (left, Miranda Meyer) and the African American Museum of Iowa (Corridor Business Journal) underwent extensive renovations after the flood.*

Above: *Bicyclists relax at Lion Bridge Brewing Company in Cedar Rapids' Czech Village (Angela Holmes).*

"SINCE THE FLOOD, THERE'S BEEN A LOT OF EMPHASIS TO HAVE MORE BUSINESSES AND THINGS TO DO DOWNTOWN. THE RESTAURANTS ARE FULL, THERE'S A LOT OF ACTIVITY AND PEOPLE REALLY WANT TO BE DOWNTOWN," SAID RANDY RAMLO, PRESIDENT AND CEO, UNITED FIRE GROUP.

An insurer takes a risk on downtown Cedar Rapids

Among those major employers is United Fire Group (UFG), a multi-billion-dollar, publicly-traded insurance company that experienced extensive flood damage at its corporate headquarters in downtown Cedar Rapids. Days before the river crested, the company was told to leave its building. Employees and volunteers spent hours sandbagging. On Wednesday, June 11, the river was lapping at the parking lot. By the next day, the basement was filling with water. The building ended up with 6 feet of water which destroyed furniture and computer equipment.

"We had a disaster plan that took care of all the big-ticket items but not the small-ticket items," said Randy Ramlo, UFG Insurance's president and CEO.

The company packed up what it could and reopened a week later at temporary office space in Norway, Iowa, 22 miles west of Cedar Rapids. Nationwide, UFG employs 1,200 people, 400 of which were working in Cedar Rapids in 2008. The Norway building was equipped with an uninterruptible power source, a necessity for the company. Employees sat at folding tables and created makeshift workspaces to handle claims, customer calls and perform accounting and other functions. There were two six-hour shifts a day to accommodate workers.

"We bussed everyone to Norway every day, picking them up at a parking lot in Cedar Rapids and taking them back," Ramlo said. "It was a great team-building exercise. Our vendors brought ice cream and we cooked burgers some days. It was a neat experience because everyone really pulled together and forgot about their differences."

UFG employees move into a temporary office in Norway, Iowa, while the company's downtown building was flooded, cleaned and renovated (United Fire Group).

Opposite: Top, a worker walks into United Fire Group's downtown headquarters to inspect flood damage; below, workers help move boxes and set up a temporary space (United Fire Group).

UFG partnered with Cedar Rapids Bank & Trust, which offered to share space with the insurer, so UFG conducted several executive meetings at the bank.

Since returning downtown in early September 2008, UFG has purchased five more downtown buildings. Among those is the historic, 10-story American Building, which served as a bank when it opened in 1914.

"It's a commitment to Cedar Rapids. We decided to show everyone we're staying here," Ramlo said. "Iowa is our most effective, efficient office. We plan to continue to grow in Iowa as much as we can."

The company decided to enter a growth mode in 2010 to protect itself from acquisitions and has achieved many successes, including improved markets and offerings. UFG is upgrading its downtown buildings and adding parking to the basements as a flood protection measure. The company will likely expand into additional buildings in the future, he said.

The city's business-friendly attitude has played a big part in UFG's commitment to downtown, he said.

"The city became much easier to work with post-flood," Ramlo said. "The city bent over backward for us and it wasn't always that way."

Opposite: *United Fire Group employees conduct business as usual out of temporary office space in Norway, Iowa, during and after the flood. The company would often host barbecue lunches at the temporary space (United Fire Group).*

Above: *United Fire Group returned to its downtown location and continues to expand (United Fire Group).*

Corridor Rising

Moving into a library creates growth

One of UFG's insurance partners, TrueNorth Companies, also made a commitment to downtown Cedar Rapids after the flood. TrueNorth, an insurance and financial services company, took on water at its corporate headquarters at Fourth Avenue and Fifth Street SE in 2008. Damage was minimal and the company was able to quickly return. Little did the insurer know then that it would play a major part in Cedar Rapids' flood recovery.

As the city proceeded with the renovation and replacement plans for several of its facilities, the public library board approached TrueNorth about swapping locations with the insurer. At first TrueNorth turned them down. But the library persisted.

After a series of discussions, TrueNorth decided to take over and renovate the downtown library's flooded building on First Avenue along the river. Adapting the flooded library into a modern office space became an exciting challenge for the company and the community.

"I underestimated the value a new facility could have on our company culture, our ability to recruit, the efficiencies and atmosphere it created," said Duane Smith, TrueNorth's CEO. "It's given us the opportunity to grow and expand. We've doubled our staff and plan to expand again."

TrueNorth worked with OPN Architects to convert the one-story library into a two-story building to protect against future flooding. As part of that protection, the first floor houses only the company's lobby and a few offices; the remainder of the first floor is now used for parking. Mechanical and electrical equipment was elevated above the 2008 flood level, and company servers are located off site. The company moved into its new building in November 2011.

TrueNorth's renovation of the library planned for future expansion into shell space, which was formerly the children's library. The extra space was a boon because in 2015, TrueNorth announced a $2 million expansion to accommodate 57 potential new jobs.

"It became a real win-win situation for everyone involved," Smith said.

TrueNorth's growth since then has garnered state and national recognition. Inc. Magazine ranked the insurer No. 4,569 on its annual 5000 list of fastest-growing private companies. Insurance Business America (IBA) in 2017 named TrueNorth among the top 45 firms to represent retail insurance agencies.

"I UNDERESTIMATED THE VALUE A NEW FACILITY COULD HAVE ON OUR COMPANY CULTURE, OUR ABILITY TO RECRUIT, THE EFFICIENCIES AND ATMOSPHERE IT CREATED," SAID DUANE SMITH, CEO, TRUENORTH, WHICH RENOVATED THE CITY'S FLOODED PUBLIC LIBRARY.

TrueNorth decided to renovate the city's former library and convert it into office space. Since doing so, the company has grown and expanded (above, William P. Buckets; below, TrueNorth).

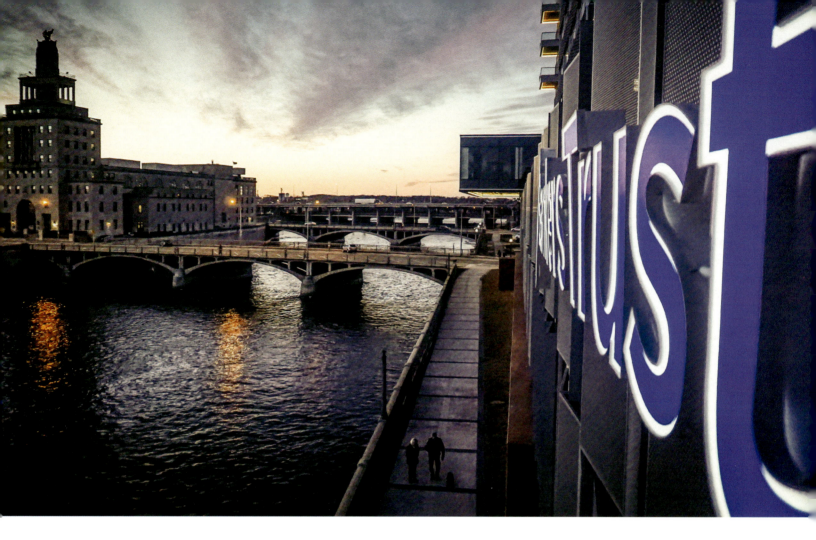

A bank invests in downtown renaissance

Another flooded company, Bankers Trust, also decided to return downtown. Its branch office, then located at the Town Centre building, 221 Third Ave. SE, took on 6 feet of water and was forced to evacuate with less than three hours' notice. Furniture, computers and files were a complete loss.

"You always have a disaster recovery plan but when a disaster actually hits, you rarely go to the disaster textbook on the shelf," said Pat Deignan, market president at Bankers Trust. "In this case, the textbook washed away down the street."

After the flood crested, Bankers Trust employees toured the branch.

"We, along with a lot of other businesses that could get to their locations via the skywalks, met up at the Five Seasons Center and walked through the skywalks in the dark with city representatives and National Guard soldiers," said Kathi Nelsen, executive assistant at Bankers Trust. "We had suitcases, wagons, recycling bins, anything we could use to carry as many things out as we could, because we didn't know when we would be allowed back in."

While the building was being cleaned and repaired, employees were reassigned to Bankers Trust's Blairs Ferry Road location.

"Banking is built on trust and access and we couldn't, and didn't, skip a beat,"

Bankers Trust moved into the CRST Center built after the flood (William P. Buckets).

Opposite: *The Bankers Trust location on Third Avenue SE received flood damage in 2008 (Bankers Trust).*

Deignan said. "We crammed 36 people into a place they didn't fit [at Blairs Ferry], but a lot of resilience and camaraderie came out of it."

Because of the tight fit, employees were sent out to visit customers, many of whom experienced flood damage themselves. Two Bankers Trust employees had flooded homes, as well, and received help from the company and their coworkers.

Four months later, after much hard work, the bank was back in its branch. Before long, Bankers Trust was invited to become part of a downtown renewal project. When CRST decided to construct an 11-story commercial building on the bank of the Cedar River, Bankers Trust joined as a tenant. The location was previously a parking ramp that had weakened during the 2008 flood.

"We weren't looking to move, we were happy where we were at," Deignan said. "But it was an opportunity for us when this building was announced. It was exciting to be part of the renaissance and making this building happen. And this is exactly what belongs here, a Class-A office building."

Bankers Trust now leases space on the 10th and 11th floors and operates a branch on the ground floor of the CRST tower. When Cedar Rapids flooded again in 2016, the company relied on lessons learned from 2008. Instead of leaving important paperwork and equipment on chairs or desks, those items were taken to the higher floors for safe keeping. The building was ultimately not affected by the 2016 flood.

"Cities need a downtown," Deignan said. "We could have left, but as a community bank, we are so intertwined with our community, and thriving communities have vibrant downtowns."

"WE, ALONG WITH A LOT OF OTHER BUSINESSES THAT COULD GET TO THEIR LOCATIONS VIA THE SKYWALKS, MET UP AT THE FIVE SEASONS CENTER AND WALKED THROUGH THE SKYWALKS IN THE DARK WITH CITY REPRESENTATIVES AND NATIONAL GUARD SOLDIERS," SAID KATHI NELSEN, EXECUTIVE ASSISTANT AT BANKERS TRUST.

Corridor Rising

Trucking company puts the pedal to the metal

CRST International decided to participate in the rebuilding of downtown Cedar Rapids after seeing the flooded river and destruction it created. Soon after the waters receded, several business leaders traveled to Grand Forks, North Dakota, which had been gutted by a flood in 1997. Cedar Rapids leaders learned many lessons on that trip: recovery can take decades, half of flooded small businesses close permanently and emergency federal funds can take a year to show up. After hearing the statistics, many of those Cedar Rapids leaders began to mobilize. Grant funding was created for nonprofits, small businesses and for the vulnerable historic neighborhoods that had been flooded. John Smith, his family and CRST generously supported these programs.

"The best thing to come out of the flood was getting these neighborhoods working together and getting things up and running again," he said.

The flood focused Smith's attention on downtown and the part his company would play in flood recovery.

"We were growing and running out of space," he said. "My dad started the business in 1955, not in Cedar Rapids but along the Lincoln Highway/Highway 30. The city grew up around us so to speak, but we've never been a downtown-oriented business. We never thought about being downtown."

For the first time in company history, CRST decided to build in the city's core. The company kept its trucks on the west side and brought its corporate offices to the new building.

"I knew I wouldn't be able to bring the operations side of the business downtown because we have to be open 24 hours, seven days a week. So, we knew it would be the corporate side. We're in three floors of this [downtown] building," Smith said. "I thought it important that we be down here, so we did it."

CRST worked with Ryan Companies to find the land and the city suggested adding flood protection to the structure. The 11-story CRST Center includes a floodwall, gatewell and pump station.

CRST demonstrated its commitment to downtown Cedar Rapids with the construction of the CRST Center (Ryan Companies; Miranda Meyer).

Opposite: The new CRST building has modern touches (Ryan Companies).

The building opened in 2016 with tenants CRST, Bankers Trust, Holmes Murphy and a four-story parking ramp, which takes up the lower levels of the structure as a flood-mitigation measure. Two weeks after moving in, the building was evacuated because of the impending September 2016 flood.

"It was easy for us (to evacuate)," Smith said. "We just picked up our computers and our phones and we walked out. Two weeks later, we walked back into the office, plugged our phones in, plugged our computers in – life was good."

As a business leader, Smith was impressed with flood prevention efforts in 2016.

"I thought the city's reaction to the 2016 flood was absolutely fantastic," he said. "I'm usually a cynic when it comes to government doing things. But I couldn't be a cynic on that one when we watched how they responded, how they got out in front of it. They were way ahead of it and they knew what was going on. They got HESCO barriers right up. And when it was over, the city employees were tired. That tells you something. It's not an 8 [a.m.] to 5 [p.m.] deal."

Before the 2008 flood, Smith had been part of a group of business leaders looking at ways to attract more residents and businesses downtown. When the flood came, the group disbanded so the community could focus on recovery.

"Before the flood, we wanted to get more people downtown, more businesses downtown, but we didn't know how to get that done," he said. "When we rebuilt downtown, this was our hope, that people would look at downtown differently. It's worked. Other businesses have moved down and the housing has increased. We're getting more businesses that are locally owned and we're seeing some mixed housing, which I love. So, I'm very bullish about downtown Cedar Rapids. We've just got to keep the pedal to the metal."

"BEFORE THE FLOOD, WE WANTED TO GET MORE PEOPLE DOWNTOWN, MORE BUSINESSES DOWNTOWN, BUT WE DIDN'T KNOW HOW TO GET THAT DONE. WHEN WE REBUILT DOWNTOWN, THIS WAS OUR HOPE: THAT PEOPLE WOULD LOOK AT DOWNTOWN DIFFERENTLY" SAID JOHN SMITH, CHAIRMAN OF THE BOARD, CRST INTERNATIONAL.

"I THINK THE REGION IS POISED TO DO SOME REALLY GREAT THINGS. WE HAVE INVESTED IN OUR CORE DISTRICTS, THE UNIVERSITY OF IOWA IS STRONGER THAN EVER, WE HAVE CONTINUED TO RECRUIT AND RETAIN COMPANIES AND SKILLED WORKFORCE AND WE CONTINUE TO BE IN A GREAT POSITION TO GROW OUR POPULATION AND OUR ECONOMY," SAID LYDIA BROWN, DIRECTOR OF REAL ESTATE, RYAN COMPANIES.

Bringing the 'grand old lady' back to life

Design and construction of the CRST Center was spearheaded by Ryan Companies, which worked with the trucking company before the flood to identify land for a new corporate building. When CRST's focus shifted to downtown, Ryan Companies worked with the city of Cedar Rapids and the U.S. Army Corps of Engineers to include a flood wall, pump station and floodable parking into the multi-tenant office structure. Ryan Companies also handled demolition of the site's parking ramp, which had been weakened by the flood. The CRST Center was among the many projects Ryan Companies worked with before, during and after the flood.

"We had a team just dedicated to flood recovery. In addition to some of the buildings that were affected by the flood, we built new facilities, as well. The CRST Tower was constructed after the flood and helped create a revised Cedar Rapids skyline," said Lydia Brown, director of real estate at Ryan Companies' Cedar Rapids office.

Ryan Companies' offices are in the GreatAmerica building, which was evacuated

CEDAR RIVER

and flooded in 2008. To help prepare for the high waters, employees helped sandbag its own building and the facilities of several other Cedar Rapids businesses, including Alliant Energy and Mercy Medical Center.

Ryan Companies also oversaw much of the post-flood construction work for the city of Cedar Rapids, including city hall, public library, fire station and Veterans Memorial Building, among others. One of the company's labors of love was the restoration of the Paramount Theatre, home to Orchestra Iowa.

"The Paramount Theatre was tragically devastated. Everything appeared to be lost but we were able to work with individuals who were able to take this historic community asset piece by piece and figure out how to reconstruct it," Brown said. "Specialists were called in both here and at Theatre Cedar Rapids to determine how these iconic buildings were built so we could rebuild them to their original glory. Our team grew in numbers and in knowledge that was directly related to the recovery of the flood."

The 1928 movie palace is listed on the National Register of Historic Places and is not only a downtown landmark, but a cherished part of Cedar Rapids' heritage. The 2008 flood caused $16 million in damage to the historic theater. At first, crews discussed demolishing the building because of the extensive damage. Everything within the theater was destroyed, including its Mighty Wurlitzer organ.

Steven Ciha, senior superintendent for Ryan Companies, was field manager in charge of the 1,700-seat theater's $35 million restoration.

"There was strong affection for the 'grand old lady' within this town that resulted in the improved renovation of the existing theater," he said. "I look back at my ignorance and think what a tragedy it would have been to destroy that building. The eyes of the city, and indeed much of Eastern Iowa, watched as we started work."

Ryan Companies coordinated the state and federal funding paperwork and requirements and combined modern and historic elements into the project. Technical components of the theater were upgraded, including its acoustics, audio/visual capabilities and stagehouse. The green room and dressing areas were elevated above flood level. Plaster was repaired and replaced throughout the theater and every inch of paint was restored to appear as it did when the theater opened in 1928.

The Paramount Theatre reopened in 2012 with its newly-restored Mighty Wurlitzer organ. The restoration project was named a 2014 Public Works Project of the Year by the American Public Works Association.

Opposite: *Construction of the CRST Center in downtown Cedar Rapids (Ryan Companies).*

Above: *The Paramount reopened in 2012 after a $35 million renovation; right, the historic building, as well as its Wurlitzer organ, was ravaged by floodwaters (Ryan Companies).*

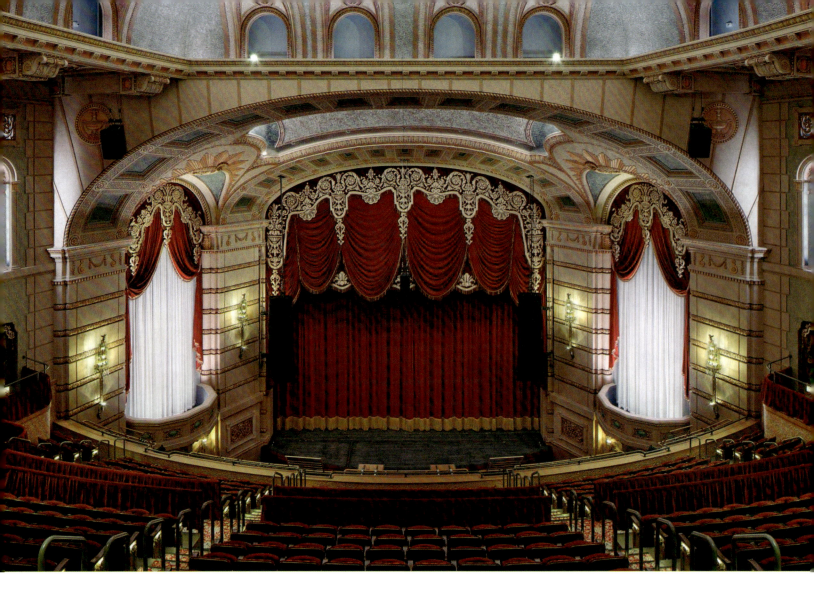

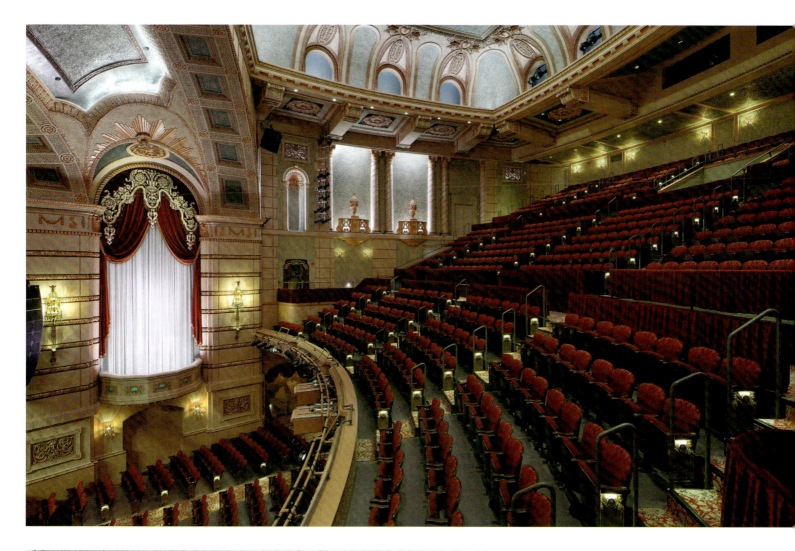

Plaster was repaired and replaced throughout the Paramount Theatre and every inch of paint was restored to appear as it did when the theater opened in 1928. The restoration project was named a 2014 Public Works Project of the Year by the American Public Works Association. (Ryan Companies).

Financial institution becomes federal expert

"THE PIPELINE OF POTENTIAL OPPORTUNITIES IS AS BIG AS IT'S EVER BEEN HERE. IT'S PRETTY EXCITING WHAT THE POSSIBILITIES ARE," SAID LARRY HELLING, PRESIDENT AND CEO, CEDAR RAPIDS BANK & TRUST.

Cedar Rapids Bank & Trust (CRBT) did not take on water in 2008, but employees watched closely as the water crept up First Avenue toward the bank's headquarters downtown. The bank was evacuated and locked out of its building for five days, so employees worked out of CRBT's Council Street branch.

"There were people out six to eight weeks with their power out, so we were very fortunate to be able to return when we did," said Larry Helling, CRBT's top executive.

When the bank was able to return, its building became a temporary home for some of its clients, including United Fire Group (UFG). CRBT is now part of UFG's disaster recovery plan, so when flood waters rose again in 2016, UFG employees set up shop in CRBT's training room.

CRBT assisted other clients, as well, helping them move furniture and equipment out of offices when flood waters rose.

In 2008, CRBT became experienced working with Federal Emergency Management Agency (FEMA) and U.S. Small Business Administration (SBA) funding applications, as many of the bank's clients needed help after the flood.

"We did a fair amount of activity with the government guarantee lenders to help people adjust to the financial impact of the flood," Helling said. "We jumped in to help clients with paperwork and the demands of government guarantee lending. Some of that gets done directly, but we helped a lot of clients navigate those waters."

CRBT now considers itself an expert in disaster funding.

"We learned a lot about those programs, which are fairly complex and we're probably the most active bank in that space in the state," he said. "We made a business out of it."

Some business customers were unable to reopen after the flood.

"There were a handful of clients who couldn't recover," Helling said. "We were aware that could happen. If you were struggling before the flood, you just might not make it."

Overall, though, the flood did have its bright spots.

"For the community, there were definitely positives. Because of the disaster recovery funds from the government, the community was able to recover in about five years instead of 25 years," he said. "That wouldn't have happened without the stimulus created by government spending, which spurred public and private funding. Another thing that came out of it were new market tax credit opportunities and historic market tax credits."

Cedar Rapids' downtown revitalization created a demand for business loans.

"The loans created momentum downtown and the momentum has created a greater need for rehab loans and new construction and we've been pretty active in that," Helling said.

While many residents and businesses have recovered since the 2008 flood, not all have.

"Generally, the economy is better than it was in 2008, unless you were one of the people flooded. If you're one of the people who had their home flooded or their businesses significantly damaged, you're certainly not better off," he said. "But that's a small segment of the population. Because of the revitalization and the general improvement in the economy since then, most people are in a better spot."

Cedar Rapids is a more entertaining and engaging place to live since the recovery and revitalization, he said.

"It feeds on itself. There are more projects coming, so more people want to live downtown and then there's more restaurants and retail; it's a snowball effect," he said. "It's great to see. The pipeline of potential opportunities is as big as it's ever been here. It's pretty exciting what the possibilities are."

Above: *A National Guard solider patrols downtown Cedar Rapids (United Fire Group).*

Health care organization bolsters partnerships, commitments

A Cedar Rapids health care organization is another business playing a major part in downtown revitalization.

Physicians Clinic of Iowa, PC, (PCI) is located at 10th Street and Second Avenue in downtown Cedar Rapids, between Unity Point Health-St. Luke's Hospital and Mercy Medical Center. The 55-block neighborhood is known as the MedQuarter Regional Medical District and the three groups work together to offer various medical services to patients. The district includes not only medical facilities, but restaurants, shops, art galleries and more. It was recently recognized by the Institute for Health Care Improvement as a top 10 city in the nation for delivering high-quality, low-cost health care.

PCI was not flooded in 2008, but the water missed the building by only 22 feet, prompting the organization to come up with a strategy to take in evacuated Mercy patients, as well as conduct reviews of its contingency plans and update its business interruption insurance.

Mike Sundall, PCI's top executive, had moved to Cedar Rapids and into a down-

town riverfront apartment just days before the flood to take on the role of PCI's CEO.

"I came to check in and the next thing I know, I'm sandbagging," he said.

Power was out downtown during the flood, so PCI needed to find alternative ways to keep medications chilled and equipment operational. Backup generators were set up and other contingency plans were put into place. They were allowed back in the building three weeks after the flood crested. PCI officials have formulated a permanent disaster plan based on lessons learned in 2008.

PCI was created in 1997 when five clinics joined together. The physicians and surgeons wanted to remain independent from the hospital systems yet share administrative and overhead to become more efficient. At the time, they remained in separate facilities and clinic offices. In 2013, the separate clinics came together under one roof with the construction of the PCI Medical Pavilion.

Patients visit PCI for various tests and treatments and are referred to specialists at the two hospitals when necessary.

"Because we are independent, we are able to partner with both Cedar Rapids' hospitals," Sundall said. "Our surgeons perform surgery in both ORs [operating rooms] and at Surgery Center Cedar Rapids, which we jointly own with St. Luke's Hospital. Additionally, some specialists travel to critical access hospitals in Anamosa, Independence, Manchester, Vinton, Sumner and Prairie du Chien, Wisconsin, where they perform surgery and/or see patients for regular appointments."

PCI also operates a location in Waterloo and treats patients at the Eastern Iowa Sleep Center in Belle Plaine.

Instead of visiting a large hospital, patients travel to PCI Medical Pavilion in downtown Cedar Rapids, where the health care facility offers covered and valet parking, concierge stations at every entrance, a coffee shop, a variety of medical specialties, lab testing and imaging and pharmacy services in one building.

"It's great, patients come in to see their physician, can get same-day testing and walk out with a prescription," Sundall said. "And the entire facility and system are built around the patient flow, the patient experience."

PCI continues to grow, acquiring various medical services and expanding its campus. One of the organization's next projects is a 98,000-square foot, three-story medical facility with a parking ramp.

"When we opened the first medical pavilion [in 2013], the intent was to fill the space over five years," he said. "It was full after just three years, making additional expansion a priority."

"I THINK THE FUTURE CAN BE VERY BRIGHT WITH THE RIGHT LEADERSHIP. FLOOD RECOVERY EFFORTS HAVE IMPROVED CITY GOVERNMENT AND WHAT'S GOING ON DOWNTOWN IS REALLY GOOD, IT'S REALLY ALIVE," SAID MIKE SUNDALL, CEO, PHYSICIANS' CLINIC OF IOWA.

Opposite: *Physicians Clinic of Iowa, PC, (PCI) is located at 10th Street and Second Avenue in downtown Cedar Rapids, between Unity Point Health-St. Luke's and Mercy hospitals.*

Above: *The 55-block neighborhood is known as the MedQuarter Regional Medical District. The district includes not only medical facilities, but restaurants, shops, art galleries and more. In 2008, flooding came within 22 feet of the PCI building (Physicians Clinic of Iowa).*

"AS DEVASTATING AS THE FLOOD WAS, IT BROUGHT THE CITY BACK TO LIFE. BUILDINGS THAT WERE EMPTY BEFORE ARE RENEWED AND FULL,"
SAID BRAD JOHNSON, VICE PRESIDENT, GENERAL MANAGER, KNUTSON CONSTRUCTION.

Sending help leads to a new Cedar Rapids office

Knutson Construction, which has operated an office in Iowa City for 40 years, sent crews to help with rising waters in Cedar Rapids.

"We all watched the news of the impending flood in 2008. These were our neighbors and we knew we needed to help, so we sent a 1-ton truck with a few employees to help with sandbagging and anything else that was needed," said Brad Johnson, vice president and general manager of Knutson Construction, Iowa City. "We sent dozens of employees who spent countless hours, blood, sweat and tears to help our friends and neighbors. Cedar Rapids is a part of who we are and we are proud to have been a part of the flood preparation and recovery of the city."

The company was contracted to work on renovation of TrueNorth's original building, converting it into space for the downtown Cedar Rapids Public Library. Ongoing flood recovery projects, coupled with downtown reinvestment and growth, led to Knutson opening an office in Cedar Rapids.

"Prior to the flood of 2008, there were few (construction) opportunities in Cedar Rapids. Since then, the city has continued to grow and flourish," Johnson said. "We built a lot of relationships with new clients, subcontractors, suppliers and developers in Cedar Rapids that are still strong today, 10 years later. We were able to assist many of those partners again during the flood of 2016."

Downtown Cedar Rapids' renewed vitality is a positive change for the entire Corridor, Johnson said.

"As devastating as the flood was, it brought the city back to life. Buildings that were empty before are renewed and full. The city has a renewed life and spirit," he said.

That renewal has extended into Cedar Rapids' downtown historic districts.

Above: *Knutson Construction was one of the companies that worked to create the library's new location (Ryan Companies).*

Opposite: *The former Cedar Rapids Library was extensively damaged in the 2008 flooding.*

New Bohemia, Czech Village and Kingston Village districts

The flooding of 2008 did more than wipe out government and business buildings. It erased large swaths of the city's heritage – its most historic and beloved neighborhoods. Cedar Rapids was incorporated in 1849 and was home to many groups of immigrants, most notably families from the Bohemia region of Czech Republic, the greater Czech Republic and Slovakia. They set up homes in downtown Cedar Rapids,

"GETTING THROUGH A DISASTER OF THIS MAGNITUDE, OUR CITY LEADERSHIP, THEY WERE CHALLENGED WITH SOMETHING THEY PROBABLY THOUGHT THEY WOULD NEVER HAVE TO DEAL WITH," SAID LURA MCBRIDE, PRESIDENT AND CEO, VAN METER INC.

creating unique, adjacent neighborhoods. As the groups migrated west across the country, many stayed in Cedar Rapids as they found ample employment in the burgeoning city's meatpacking plants and factories.

The Sinclair meatpacking plant opened in 1871, becoming a major employer in the area and a downtown fixture until it closed in 1990. When it opened, it was the fourth-largest meatpacking plant in the world. The owner, T.M. Sinclair, died in a workplace fall and his widow, Caroline Sinclair, built a 26-acre estate to raise their six children. The estate, now known as Brucemore, a museum and community gathering center, hosted Orchestra Iowa's post-flood comeback concert in the fall of 2008 to a standing-room-only crowd. Orchestra Iowa's home, the Paramount Theatre, was one of the downtown cultural landmarks flooded in 2008.

Today, New Bohemia, Czech Village, Kingston Village and main downtown districts are once again catalysts of the city's growth. While these neighborhoods experienced

NewBo City Market is a hub of activity in downtown Cedar Rapids' New Bohemia District, such as the NewBo Run (Calcam AP, LLC).

Corridor Rising

Above: *NewBo City Market (John Richard); Czech Village (Angela Holmes); Raygun's New Bohemia District store (Gigi Wood). Right, the NewBo City Market is a popular spot to shop or grab something to eat (John Richard).*

Below: *The National Czech & Slovak Museum & Library underwent a $25 million restoration, renovation and expansion, including the move and elevation of the building after it filled with 8 feet of water in 2008 (John Richard).*

Opposite: *Top, New Bohemia Houby Days Parade (Cindy Hadish). Right, CSPS Hall (Corridor Business Journal), The Depot (Corridor Business Journal) and Water Tower Place (Brian Draeger).*

severe damage, neighborhood, community and business leaders were determined to restore and improve these districts on both sides of the river.

"It was sad to see the houses in the Time Check neighborhood destroyed. A lot of those people were retired, on limited incomes and lost everything they had," Van Meter's Dave Klostermann said. "The neat thing today is to go down to places like [the New Bohemia District] and see the improvements that have been made, the things people have done to physically make the area better, but also to make the city a neater place to be."

The most notable change in NewBo since the flood is the emergence of NewBo City Market, a nonprofit, indoor public market full of several small vendors. The $4 million project built where a former Quality Chef Foods plant was located has become a favorite gathering spot for the community and a popular tourist destination. The zero-waste market incorporates sustainability practices, from rain barrels that water the outdoor gardens to electric car charging stations. Shops include a coffee house, bakery, beer and wine store, soap maker and variety of food vendors. The outdoor market yard is a hot spot for live music, yoga classes and other community events.

Next door is The Depot, a $17 million mixed-use development with retail, office and apartments. The new building was constructed on the site of the former Iowa Steel and Iron Works paving-equipment company, dating back to the 1920s.

Across the street is the headquarters of Geonetric, a health care marketing company and various business startup centers. The building was constructed at the site of the former Star Wagon Works, an 1800s-era wagon factory.

Environmental remediation was conducted on the former factory sites, with funding help from local, state and federal sources. NewBo's projects received a Phoenix Award from the Phoenix Awards Institute, which recognizes outstanding achievement and innovation relating to environmental and community issues.

Nearby, companies that have become local favorites include The Pig & Porter and Parlor City restaurants, Next Page Books, t-shirt shop Raygun and coffee stop Brewhemia. The CSPS Hall, dating back to 1890, is home to nonprofit arts organization Legion Arts and received a major renovation.

Two major renovation projects in Czech Village include:

National Czech & Slovak Museum & Library, which underwent a $25 million restoration, renovation and expansion, including the move and elevation of the building after it filled with 8 feet of water in 2008.

The African American Museum of Iowa was the first nonprofit to return to its restored building, after it experienced $1.3 million in damage.

The neighborhood is home to a new brewery, Lion Bridge Brewing, and several established favorites, such as the Sykora Bakery, Czech Cottage, Czech Village Antiques, Dostal Catering and White Lion Treasures.

Home to the McGrath Amphitheatre, Kingston Village features new, upscale residential spaces, such as The Metropolitan and Kingston Village Apartments. Popoli Ristorante & Sullivan's Bar opened in the renovated People's Bank, a historic Louis Henry Sullivan bank built in 1912. Several local favorites reopened after the flood. Office supply shop Office Express, outdoor power equipment store Sled Shed and hot dog eatery the Flying Wienie were among the many small businesses to evacuate and then return to the neighborhood after the flood.

In the Time Check neighborhood, the Mother Mosque of America, known as the oldest "standing purpose-built" mosque in the country, was extensively damaged during the flood, as its documents and artifact were destroyed. Through much community support, the mosque was able to recover.

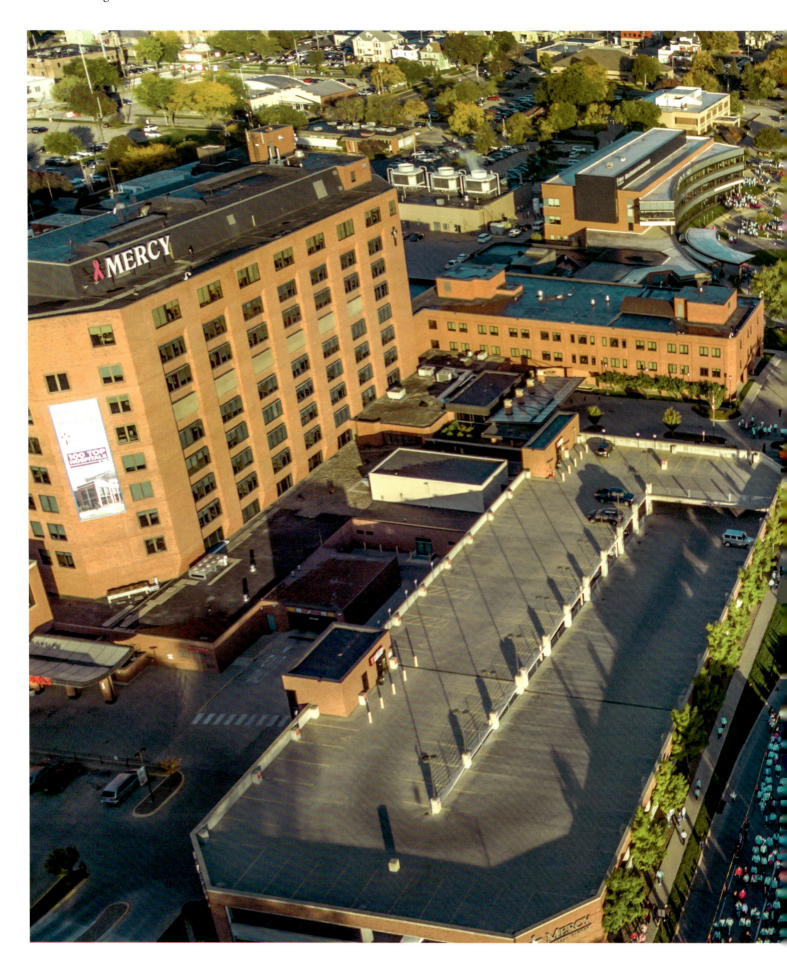

Especially for You Race near Mercy Medical Center in Cedar Rapids (Calcam AP, LLC).

Creating a prosperous future/Looking ahead

"THE CEDAR RAPIDS/IOWA CITY CORRIDOR IS WORKING TOGETHER TO ENSURE OUR ECONOMY CONTINUES TO GROW AND THRIVE AND OUR COMPANIES ARE ABLE TO FIND AND RETAIN THE TALENT THEY NEED TO STAY HERE," SAID JENNIFER DALY, PRESIDENT AND CEO, JOINT VENTURE, CEDAR RAPIDS/IOWA CITY CORRIDOR DEVELOPMENT CORP.

Cedar Rapids was named National Civic League's All America City 2014. The award recognizes communities where citizens work to identify and overcome city-wide challenges and achieve uncommon results. The Cedar Rapids application focused on the city's goal of rebuilding a healthier community after the flood, using three pillars: neighborhood revitalization, commitment to arts and culture, and creating a culture of health and well-being.

Today, the city of 256,000 people is a hotbed of growth and opportunity. It has racked up many rankings on national surveys during recent years, including:

No. 1 place to raise a child for three years in a row
No. 1 best small city to live and work
No. 2 among top places for teachers
No. 3 among happiest cities in America
No. 3 town where poverty is falling fastest
No. 4 among best cities
No. 5 best city for millennials to "get rich"
No. 6 among best American cities for technology workers and named a Google eCity
No. 6 best city for living the American dream
No. 7 for best commute
No. 7 best city to make a living
No. 9 healthiest small city in America
No. 11 for best city services
No. 19 among the best run cities in America.
One of the top 10 most affordable places to live.

Given these accolades, it's no surprise the city and surrounding areas have grown during the past decade. Cedar Rapids' population has increased 6 percent, while adjacent communities such as Hiawatha, Marion and Robins have grown 8 percent, 26 percent and 52 percent, respectively.

With the lowest unemployment rate since before the 2008 flood, city and business leaders are working to welcome additional workers and employers to town.

"Of all the places I've worked across the country, Cedar Rapids has been the easiest to acclimate to; people have been so friendly and approachable," said Mike Sundall of PCI, who was recruited to his position because of his breadth of health care administration experience. "My wife and I love all the wonderful restaurants downtown, as well as throughout the city."

With most of its flood-recovery projects complete, city and business leaders have changed their focus to economic development. As part of that effort, they hired a team to head up Joint Venture, whose goal is to attract skilled workforce and new

businesses to Eastern Iowa.

"The Cedar Rapids/Iowa City Corridor is working together to ensure our economy continues to grow and thrive and our companies are able to find and retain the talent they need to stay here, while continuing to add new opportunities by welcoming new employers with good, quality jobs," said Jennifer Daly, president and CEO, Joint Venture, Cedar Rapids/Iowa City Corridor Development Corp.

The team is working to promote the region to site selection companies and targeting specific industry clusters for growth. Daly has planned more than 20 business trips in 2018 to promote the Corridor.

"We'll be sharing our story and gathering business intelligence for different industries," she said.

The group is also working with local businesses, schools and others to enhance the region's talent pipeline. Students in K-12 will receive help developing their career plans.

"We'll be helping students make great decisions for their futures and show them local opportunities based on the needs of employers," Daly said. "From that we'll create a talent forecast based on who employers are planning to hire and what their biggest needs are."

Alumni from the many area colleges and universities will be invited back to help fill positions.

"We will be successful when our economy continues to grow and thrive and when our companies are able to find and retain the talent they need to be able to stay and grow here," Daly said.

Above: *Nelly concert at the McGrath Amphitheatre (William P. Buckets).*

Corridor Rising

Nelly packs in a crowd at the McGrath Amphitheatre which was built along the Cedar River after the flood (William P. Buckets).

Opposite: *Top, drone photo of Cedar Rapids flooding (Corridor Business Journal); bottom, boat travels along the Cedar River (William P. Buckets).*

Concert outside of NewBo City Market (Calcam AP, LLC).

Flood waters continue south through Sutliff, southeast Iowa

Above and left: *Sutliff Bridge and the neighboring Baxa's Sutliff Store and Tavern are popular stops for motorcyclists and bicyclists (Baxa's Sutliff Store and Tavern).*

In June 2008, flood waters continued past Cedar Rapids, causing damage to communities downstream. One such community is Sutliff, an unincorporated town of 57 people southeast of Cedar Rapids and Mount Vernon. Sutliff is home to a historic 1897 truss bridge that was a favorite spot for bicyclists and motorcyclists. The adja-

cent Baxa's Sutliff Store and Tavern, which originally opened in the 1800s as a general store, would host travelers and trail riders during warm months, who enjoyed beverages along the rural and scenic stretch of the river. The bridge washed away during the 2008 flood.

Named to the National Registry of Historic Places in 1998, Johnson County officials decided to rebuild the bridge after the flood. Community groups raised donations and FEMA granted $1.3 million for the project, which was completed in 2012. The bridge, store and trails attract thousands of tourists annually.

Surging water weaved its way through farming communities in Eastern Iowa until it arrived at the Cedar River's end in Columbus Junction and Fredonia. Homes and businesses were inundated with as much as 10 feet of water in those towns, which are located at the conflux of the Cedar and Iowa rivers. The Cedar River ends at this point, emptying into the Iowa River. The surge went on to deluge several more small Iowa towns, including Oakville, before meeting up with the Mississippi River. Flooding hit Illinois and Missouri, moving along the Mighty Mississippi before it eventually dissipated into the Gulf of Mexico at the end of June 2008.

Aerial view of the University of Iowa campus, Art Building West in foreground (University of Iowa).

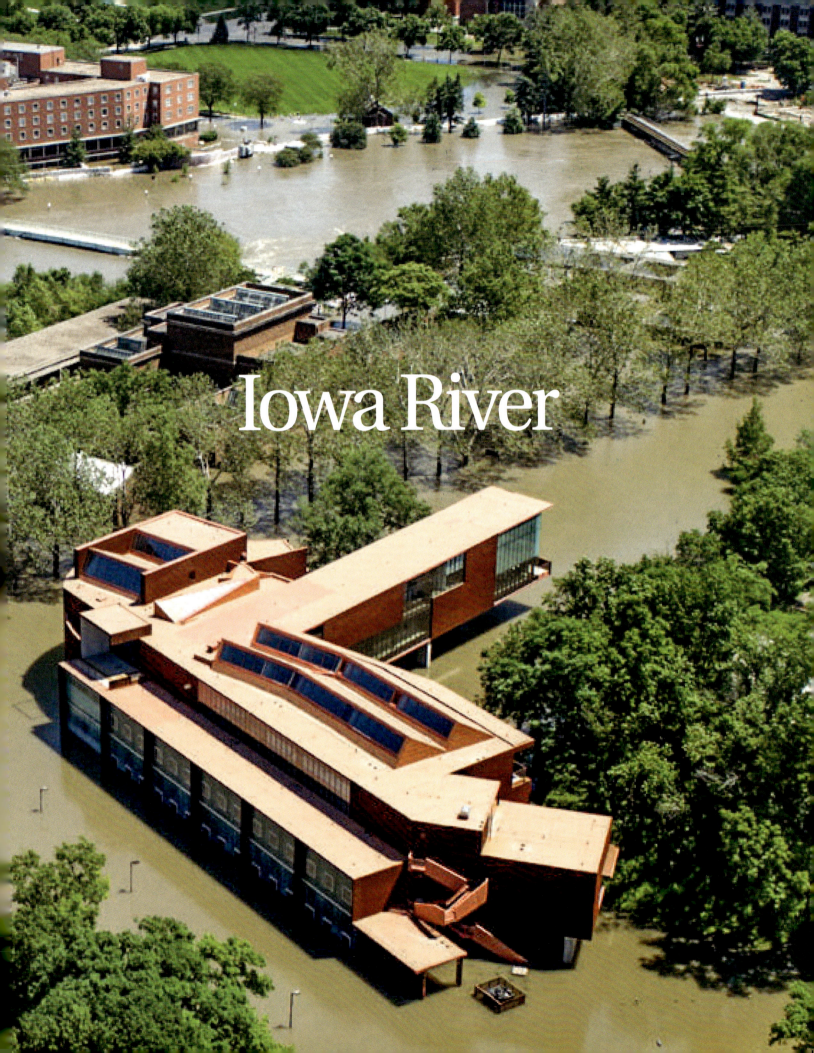
Iowa River

Heavy snowfall followed by a wet spring

Just as the Cedar River basin had experienced unusually heavy snow and rain seasons during the winter and spring of 2007-2008, so, too, did the Iowa River. The two rivers run parallel to one another from north-central Iowa to the southeast part of the state, before emptying into the Mississippi River.

The high waters that surged along the Cedar River followed a similar journey along the Iowa River. Major storms passing through the northern part of the state overflowed the tributaries leading to the Iowa River. Flooding began in Belmond, a town of 2,300 west of Interstate 35 near Mason City. Basements filled with water in homes and businesses and the city's storm sewer system was overwhelmed.

From there, flooding traveled along the Iowa River through several small towns in central Iowa, reaching record levels along the way and submerging thousands of acres of farmland. In Iowa Falls, 14 inches of rain fell in a 16-day span. The city's airport runway, public library and sewer system were flooded. A 1920s-era concrete arch bridge along Highway 65 was heavily damaged in the flood and when it was repaired, it was outfitted with sensors and other gauges to monitor vehicle traffic and river levels.

At the flood's next stop in Marshalltown, bridges, roads, rail lines and trails were also damaged. Highway 14 was one of many roads in the region overtaken by the river and closed. The river crested at 21.79 feet, topping the previous record of 20.77 feet in 1993. Alliant Energy shut down its Sutherland Generating Station as a precautionary measure, affecting 2,600 customers. Located a quarter mile from the river, the generating station took on 4 inches of water and was offline for two weeks. The coal plant has since been replaced by a natural gas power plant. Similar to neighboring towns, some houses and businesses took on water in basements. The city and county invested in various flood mitigation measures, such as improving roads and culverts.

Flooding continued south of Marshalltown, where a historic truss bridge in Le Grand was destroyed by high water.

The river crested at 21.30 feet on June 13 in Tama, extensively damaging the Meskwaki Settlement of the Sac and Fox tribes. The groups' popular, annual powwow event was moved to an alternate location as a result. Throughout Tama County, roads, bridges and farms were damaged by the flood.

Extending eastward, several creeks and other tributaries connect to the Iowa River, which added to the high-water level. Thirty miles east of Tama, in Marengo, flooding increased in intensity as creeks met up with the river, where it peaked at 21.38 feet. The flood surge continued east, through the Amana Colonies and on to Coralville Lake.

Left: *Le Grand Truss Bridge destroyed by flooding (Greg Hall).*

Coralville Dam and Reservoir

The Iowa River winds its way through the Hawkeye Wildlife Management Area near Swisher before reaching Coralville Lake, north of North Liberty. The 23-mile-long lake is part of a 5,280-acre recreation area and dam system that includes camping, fishing, trails and the Devonian Fossil Gorge, a 375-million-year-old fossil bed exposed by the 1993 floods.

The Coralville Reservoir and Dam were constructed in 1958 to reduce flooding from the Iowa River into the Mississippi. The dam is 1,400 feet long and 100 feet high. A spillway is connected to the dam and is designed to release overflow water during flooding events or to release water during times of drought. The spillway is positioned 712 feet above sea level.

On June 10, the river did the unthinkable and overflowed the spillway. Typically, river outflow at the dam is 3,700 cubic feet per second (cfs). On June 15, the dam recorded its highest outflow ever, at 39,500 cfs and 717 feet.

As the flood gained speed and breadth, no one was expecting the damage it would cause. From damages to repairs, the flooding cost roughly $1 billion in Coralville and Iowa City.

Despite the debilitating billions of dollars of damage the overflow caused downstream, the Army Corps of Engineers estimates the presence of the Coralville Reservoir and Dam prevented $66 million in more damage during the 2008 flood.

"Usually the flooding happens earlier in the spring when you have snowmelt in the Iowa River watershed that tends to raise the levels and we try to control that at the reservoir," said Dale Helling, who worked for the city of Iowa City for 36 years until he retired in 2011. At the time of the flood, he served as assistant city manager. "When you get past the spring, you sort of breathe easy. All of a sudden, we were in a situation where we were gearing up after we thought we had already dodged the flood for that year."

Typically, flooding patterns come with more predictability than it did in 2008.

"In the spring, you know how much snowfall has occurred, you know how much snow is on the ground upstream and in the watershed, so you can calculate all those things and factor in how much rain you normally get in the spring to make predictions and prepare for it that way. For this [2008 floods], almost every day we were hoping, even with all the rainfall, we could get away without having a flood. But the predictions kept going up. And when the water goes over the spillway, then it's out of control."

Devonian Fossil Gorge, which was unearthed by flooding in 1993 (City of Coralville).

Coralville

The flood's next stop was Coralville. For weeks, the region had experienced bursts of flash flooding mixed with afternoons of sunshine, during which residents sandbagged. Thousands of volunteers filled and placed more than 6 million sandbags along the Iowa River in Johnson County. Most sandbag walls were built to the 1993 flood elevation, at 28.52 feet. The river, however, crested at 31.53 feet on June 15.

Residents and business owners in Coralville spent the week of June 9 anxiously checking weather reports and updates from the Army Corps of Engineers and local news stations. Flood predictions changed frequently. Although the spillway over-

Volunteers fill sandbags and build walls around important infrastructure during the days leading up to the flooding of 2008 (City of Coralville).

flowed on Tuesday, June 10, a string of sun-filled afternoons had been reassuring. It came as a surprise when National Guard soldiers left mandatory evacuation notices on homes and businesses along the city's busiest business district and nearby neighborhoods.

Soon, the river began to noticeably rise by the hour, flowing into parking lots. It became a last-minute scramble to protect keepsakes in homes and inventory in businesses. Expecting no more than a few inches of water, chairs were put on tables, power cords were unplugged and if possible, appliances and equipment were elevated.

The storms returned in earnest. Days were filled with rain and nights were filled with thunder and lightning. By Thursday, June 12, water reduced traffic lanes on Highway 6, Coralville's busiest thoroughfare. On Friday, June 13, it was clear the flood was staggeringly more intense than expected. Residents were advised to leave the region, if possible, as roads were quickly being overtaken by the river.

Throughout eastern Iowa, roads were closed in every direction. Detours diverted drivers – hours and at times, hundreds of miles – off course. Even in the Coralville/

Opposite: *Top, residents are evacuated by boat (U.S. Geological Survey); bottom, cars and homes were submerged by the Iowa River (City of Coralville).*

Above: *Highway 6 was flooded, blocking access to hospitals and the University of Iowa campus (City of Coralville).*

Iowa City area, roads were difficult to navigate. So many streets were flooded and closed between the two cities, some residents were unable to travel to work, grocery stores and other locations.

At Interstate 80 and First Avenue, known as the Iowa River Landing District, the river rose to the steps of the Coralville Marriott Hotel and Conference Center, built just two years earlier. The hotel was unharmed, but the homes between the hotel and the river were inundated. No one was injured, although most of the properties were severely damaged.

The city of Coralville later invested in several home buyouts in the district. That land is now greenspace to help dissipate future flooding and the city has built an earthen berm with a trail along the river. The 180-acre Iowa River Landing District has been booming ever since, and is now home to Trader Joe's, Von Maur, J. Jill, Lululemon, a major medical clinic, upscale apartments, another modern hotel and restaurants. Future plans for the district include a $46 million arena, as well as additional medical clinics, stores and restaurants.

Back in 2008, floodwaters advanced past the Iowa River Landing District, swelling over the riverbanks into businesses and across roads at the landmark Iowa River Power Restaurant.

Just south of the IRP, the river meets up with Clear Creek. At this spot, trees and debris picked up by the river slammed into an essential railroad bridge and road. The resulting bottleneck increased flooding in the area.

Water levels rose at an alarming rate along Clear and Biscuit creeks, filling businesses and apartment buildings with as much as 9 feet of water. Roads were impassable. Floodwaters were so high, the nearby First Avenue/Highway 6 intersection – the busiest in the county – was under water for 10 days.

Along the Iowa River and city creeks, 200 businesses were damaged or destroyed, from Mekong Asian Restaurant to Wig and Pen, home of the Flying Tomato pizza.

Mekong, which had been flooded in 1993, did not return to its Coralville location after the 2008 event. The business instead reopened in Iowa City, building it into a successful restaurant before the owners retired in 2016.

Opposite: *Flooding at the Coralville Marriott Hotel and Conference Center and, above, along Highway 6 in Coralville (City of Coralville).*

The flooding headed west along the Coralville Strip, inundating restaurant chains like Hardee's, Taco John's and Lone Star Steakhouse. Hardee's demolished its restaurant at the busy intersection of Highway 6 and First Avenue. Franchise owner Lee Staak decided to elevate the property and rebuild. Next door, Dave Sondag's barber shop was submerged with 4 feet of water. While it was being gutted and rebuilt, Sondag cut hair in his garage. He later returned to the building where he worked until he retired in 2012. Lone Star Steakhouse did not reopen.

The river crossed Highway 6, making it impassable, and decimated Frohwein Office Plus, a fourth-generation, family-owned company. Its showroom and inventory of office furniture and supplies were destroyed. The company was able to recover, however, and has since expanded and merged with Pioneer Workspace Solutions to become Tallgrass Business Resources.

On the east side of First Avenue, south of Iowa River Power Restaurant, was Taco Bell. The fast food chain was next to the juncture of the Iowa River, Clear Creek and CRANDIC railroad bridge and filled with several feet of water. The building was demolished, and several flood mitigation measures were added to the property. A very

"THINGS ARE GOING TO CONTINUE TO IMPROVE. BOTH IOWA CITY AND CORALVILLE ARE REALLY LOOKING AT THE RIVER AND WHAT WE CAN DO ALONG THE RIVERFRONT," SAID KELLY HAYWORTH, CITY ADMINISTRATOR, CITY OF CORALVILLE.

busy Panera Bread is now located on the property. Taco Bell has since relocated.

The flood overtook the railroad bridge and embankment, which served as berm protecting the surrounding businesses. Water entered several businesses in a strip mall next door, filling them up to 9 feet. It went on to fill Peking Buffet and Old Chicago with 6 feet of water. Old Chicago owner Joe McLaughlin later lamented spending time sandbagging when, he said, time would have been better spent evacuating equipment and furniture. Peking Buffet demolished its building and reopened three years later after elevating its property. A few doors east, the Vine Tavern & Eatery took on 4 feet of water and reopened a few months later.

Wig and Pen owner Dick Querry decided to rebuild after the restaurant filled with nearly 7 feet of water. The business spent several months gutting and renovating, and on FEMA's insistence, built a permanent floodwall around the building. Since the flood, Wig and Pen has expanded and recently opened a fourth location in North Liberty.

Across the street, floral shop Every Bloomin' Thing filled with 4 feet of water. Before the flood, mother-daughter team Sanja Hunt and Maja Hunt moved as many flowers, vases and other equipment as they could out of the building. Each day, the river moved ominously closer as it crept along Rocky Shore Drive. The

From top left clockwise: *Hardee's, Wig and Pen Pizza Pub, Randy's Carpets and Interiors, Days Inn & Suites, Sonic Drive-In and Peking Buffet (City of Coralville).*

"A YEAR AFTER THE FLOOD, ONLY 50 PERCENT OF BUSINESSES HAD RETURNED. THAT'S WHY WE'VE DONE SO MUCH WITH FLOOD PROTECTION, SO THEY NEVER HAVE TO GO THROUGH THAT AGAIN," SAID ELLEN HABEL, ASSISTANT CITY ADMINISTRATOR, CITY OF CORALVILLE.

flood destroyed more than expected and it took months to rebuild and reopen. But the Hunts returned with their own clever flood mitigation measures. After gutting their building, they installed concrete flooring, and all the tables and workspaces are on wheels. If floodwater reaches their building again, they will be able to make a hasty escape. Wiring for electrical and phone systems was elevated, as well.

Along the way, water pushed through countless other businesses, including Coral Lanes bowling alley, a furniture store, scrapbooking store, hotel, church, auto body shop, a major copy and printing business and more. For some, it was a six-figure loss. A few were near retirement and chose not to reopen. A year later, 50 percent of the impacted businesses still had not reopened.

Slugger's Neighborhood Grill

One of those flooded businesses was Slugger's Neighborhood Grill, a sports bar and restaurant along Highway 6. Faye Swift opened the restaurant in 1988, back when it was more difficult for a woman to secure a business loan. In the days before the flood, Swift had been going about business as usual, all while keeping an eye on the rising creek behind her building.

Her family and coworkers built a sandbag wall around the building and were ready with pumps if the water broke through.

"The day before the flood, my brother was in town." Swift recalled. "We were standing on the back of the creek and we were saying, 'it's not going to flood, it's not going to flood.'"

The night before water entered the restaurant, they felt confident the building would be fine.

"The next day it was over by the Power Company [restaurant], slowly coming up into their parking lot. And it started raining," Swift said. "At about 9 at night, it was pouring rain and thundering and MidAmerican Energy came around and said, 'we're going to shut your power down, it's time for you to go.'"

They gave away the food and beer in the coolers, knowing it would be spoiled by morning. She headed home with her son, Matt Swift, who also worked at the restaurant.

"When they told us they were going to turn the power off and told me to lock the door, I felt like I was abandoning a child. I was leaving my baby I had had for 20 years," she said. "Then the next day, we drove down to get as close as we could, and we got out of the car and waded through the water, over by Randy's Carpets."

The water was only about a foot deep at that time.

"I thought, this isn't so bad," she said. "And then the next day we went back, and it was like this high [3 feet]. And that's when I knew."

The family was unable to officially return to the building for two weeks. That's how long the water sat, stagnating. Generally, when water is higher than 4 inches in a building, everything needs to be torn out and replaced, including flooring, drywall, wiring and more. But when the water receded, Matt was determined to clean and reopen the restaurant with his family and friends.

"I remember how naïve I was, because I went to the store and bought tools and thought I was going to go in there and chop it all up and take it all out, and it was going to be great," he said. "About an hour into that project, I realized I didn't know what I was doing. Everything was ruined and needed to be mitigated. And there's a whole process to that and you become aware of that quickly."

Crews were brought in to help with the cleanup and mitigation. At that point, Faye Swift was trying to decide whether to stay in business. She eventually chose to pursue

Slugger's Neighborhood Grill, a sports bar and restaurant, was open for 20 years along Highway 6 before it flooded in 2008. Owner Faye Swift chose not to reopen at that location, but, along with a business partnership, opened restaurants in North Liberty, Solon, Iowa City and Coralville's Iowa River Landing District (City of Coralville).

the FEMA disaster loans available to flooded business, offered at an interest rate of 4 percent.

FEMA had set up an office at the county fairgrounds, so she collected all the required paperwork and took it in.

"I thought I was never going to go into the restaurant business again, but I stayed on course with FEMA with the loan. I kept thinking, 'what if' and 'no, I'm not going to do it,'" she said. "I went to the fairgrounds with my box of paperwork and I said, 'I'm here to apply for the 4 percent loan to get back into business.' The lady said, 'well, it requires a lot of papers.' And I said, 'I know,' and I put the box down. And I told her, 'this is everything you asked for.' And she said, 'you're one of the first.'"

At the time of the flood, the Swift family ran Slugger's in Coralville and Blackstone Fine Dining in Iowa City, which was one of the first sit-down restaurants to open on the fast-growing east side of town. They decided not to reopen Slugger's.

Not too long after the flood, they found a new place to set up. Rookie's Fine Food & Spirits closed in North Liberty, and the building, 6 miles north of Slugger's, became available. They used the FEMA loan to open Reds Alehouse, a restaurant that serves more than 150 microbrews.

"This [Reds building] came up for sale and everything changed," she said.

Faye Swift was back in the restaurant business.

"I used to drive by [Reds] all the time thinking, 'that's the cutest building,'" she said. "Then it came for sale and people were calling me saying, 'you should get that.' And then I did."

Many of the staff who had worked at Slugger's followed the Swifts to Reds when it opened. Some of them have gone on to manage and own restaurants started by the Swift family, including Big Grove Brewpub in Solon, 30hop in Coralville, Mosley's Barbecue and Provisions, Pullman Bar & Diner and Big Grove Brewery & Taproom in

Iowa City's Riverfront Crossings District. Matt Swift also bought Atlas Restaurant in downtown Iowa City. The family co-owns the restaurants with several business partners, many of whom worked at Slugger's.

"It is a lot of work, but if it's the right people involved, it takes a lot of the work away," he said. "If you have a team that's strong and you have the financial backing and most importantly, the talent, you can always figure out the rest of the details. And everyone here is driven to do great things."

Matt Swift credits his mother's resilience after the flood, and during the flood itself, with the family's continued business success.

"Her fortitude is what made it all happen. She kept on that FEMA thing. Had she not done that, Reds would never have happened. Then the rest wouldn't have happened," he said. "It almost feels guided at some point."

Reds Alehouse has become a focal point of neighborhood activity in North Liberty's burgeoning downtown.

"We've always really liked the concept of being in the heart of the community," he said. "We're right in the middle of Solon. And when you go to Google North Liberty, the star is right on top of Reds. It's the heart of the community and we're big believers in that Main Street effect."

While the flood was devastating, it also sparked a lot of good, they said.

"When we opened Blackstone, I was 55 years old," Faye Swift said. "So, all my major successes in life have been from 55 and on."

Opposite: *Slugger's took on more than 3 feet of water in 2008 (City of Coralville).*

Above: *Slugger's owner Faye Swift, decided to not reopen the restaurant but later opened Reds Alehouse in North Liberty (Corridor Business Journal).*

Coralville rolls up its sleeves

After the flood waters receded, cleanup of businesses along First Avenue and Highway 6 began. Industrial-size dumpsters were a common sight along the Coralville Strip, as business owners threw away nearly everything. Many, when reminiscing about the flood, will remark how it wasn't the destroyed tables, chairs and countertops that were missed. Instead, it was all the little things – the "good" stapler, the company logo stamp, the knickknacks next to the register, the list of phone numbers and to-dos – that were impossible to replace. In 2008, apps and cloud-based services were not as common as they are today; notes on paper were used most often.

Similar to cleanup efforts in Cedar Rapids, professional cleanup crews went from business to business to power wash the river silt and mud. Those who experienced the flood first-hand remember how the muck left behind had a slick, oily residue on

Above: *City of Coralville officials discuss flood mitigation efforts in 2008 (City of Coralville).*

Opposite: *Several city transit and maintenance facilities were damaged by the flooding (City of Coralville).*

top of a thick, muddy bottom layer, perfect for trapping work boots.

Once clean, everything was wet. For days as businesses were closed, the loud whir of fans could be heard up and down Coralville's business district. Sometimes, the work was for naught. Several businesses ended up demolishing and rebuilding at higher elevations. If a business was assessed with 50 percent or more damage, it had to be elevated above the floodplain to receive a building permit. This rule was enforced so the city could maintain good standing with federal regulations related to disaster relief funding. To help stimulate businesses to return to the area, the state offered six months free rent.

During the days and weeks immediately following the flood, a variety of services became available. The United Way of Johnson & Washington Counties provided help to residents, while the Iowa City Area Chamber of Commerce partnered with the Community Foundation of Johnson County and the cities to distribute forgivable grants to small businesses. That assistance brought the community an important step closer to recovery.

"It was all about communication and partnerships," said Nancy Quellhorst, former president and CEO of the Iowa City Area Chamber of Commerce, who is now director of development of the University of Iowa Foundation. "We were the conduit between businesses and the resources businesses needed. We made sure our businesses in Iowa City and Coralville along the river were well informed."

Chamber staff received flood updates from Johnson County Emergency Management officials and went door to door to determine what help small businesses needed.

"As the river peaked, we visited in person every business in the flooded area to see if they were damaged and how we could assist," Quellhorst said. "We partnered with KCRG and the Gazette to create a database of the resources they needed – building supplies, cleaning equipment, tools, storage, signage, those sorts of things."

The chamber hosted a tax seminar for flooded businesses and helped organize volunteers while the Greater Iowa City Area Home Builders Association kept them apprised of reputable construction companies for restoration and rebuilding work. Chamber employees called elected officials to request assistance and to begin the process of funding applications with federal agencies such as FEMA.

The chamber also distributed $325,000 in small business grants to help companies reopen. The grants, $5,000 each, were distributed to 64 businesses for cleanup and inspections.

"It was just so important because these small businesses operate on already small margins, and then all their property loss was amplified by the business disruption. Their income diminishes or ceases for the period of time it takes them to reconstruct," Quellhorst said. "It was so heartening the way the businesses reacted. For some, it was more about having someone care, than it was about the money. It was just so hard when they kept getting bad news after bad news, going through all the inventory that had been lost, their physical infrastructure that needed to be reconstructed. Hearing that someone cared and was there to help was just huge."

"ALL OF OUR FLOOD PROTECTION IMPROVEMENTS HAVE BEEN DESIGNED TO PROTECT THE CITY FROM FUTURE FLOODS EQUAL TO THE 2008 FLOOD ELEVATION PLUS 1 FOOT," SAID DAN HOLDERNESS, CITY ENGINEER, CITY OF CORALVILLE.

Rebuilding, floodproofing begins

The city of Coralville immediately began pursuing state and federal grant funding to restore its infrastructure. Support came from Community Development Block Grants, state I-JOBS funding and from the U.S. Economic Development Administration, state sales tax proceeds, the U.S. Department of Housing and Urban Development and Federal Emergency Management Agency financing.

Like the sentiment in Cedar Rapids, the mindset became focused on not simply replacing what was lost but improving business districts and residential neighborhoods.

"From the beginning it was not about rebuilding but building back better and the council was committed to that," said Ellen Habel, the city of Coralville's assistant city administrator. "It was so important to get that permanent flood protection in place, so businesses, and everyone, knew they would never have to go through that again."

Since 2008, more than $64 million has been spent on flood repairs and protection.

"The city is much better protected now from future Iowa River, Clear Creek and Biscuit Creek flooding than in 2008," said Dan Holderness, Coralville's city engineer. "All of our flood protection improvements have been designed to protect the city from future floods equal to the 2008 flood elevation [essentially a 500-year flood] plus 1 foot. Our consultants have been very innovative with regard to the types of flood protection measures provided to make sure they fit the particular situation."

The city's top priorities were repairing and replacing the bridges and roads where the Iowa River meets Clear Creek. Projects include:

First Avenue Bridge over Clear Creek was elevated and expanded to include five lanes, 10-foot-wide sidewalks on both sides and a 10-foot-wide trail underneath.

First Avenue from the new Clear Creek bridge to south of Sixth Street was expanded to include five lanes of traffic, 10-foot-wide sidewalks on both sides and an improved storm sewer system.

Ten storm water pump stations are in place, which can pump rising water out to Clear Creek and the Iowa River. The stations can be controlled from the Wastewater Treatment Plant Control Room and have backup generator power if electrical power supplies are interrupted.

The city worked with the CRANDIC rail line to raise and rebuild the railroad bridge damaged in 2008. The elevation of Coralville bridges is a major step in the city's flood mitigation plan. At higher elevations, the bridges will be at less risk of debris obstructions, reducing flooding within the city.

Full-height earthen flood berms were added at the Iowa River Landing south of Interstate 80, along the Iowa River and Clear Creek south of the MidAmerican Energy Electrical Substation, Clear and Biscuit creeks and along the CRANDIC railroad.

A combination of permanent flood walls built to the 100-year flood elevation, plus

1 foot, and removable flood wall panels were installed along the Iowa River and its creeks.

"This combination maintains visual access to the Iowa River and Clear Creek from these properties, while providing immediate flood protection from the 100-year flood," Holderness said. "We typically are given five to seven days warning from the U.S. Army Corps of Engineers of an Iowa River flood; this allows us time to erect the removable flood wall panels if the prediction is that they will be needed. The removable flood wall panels can be staged – a certain height can be erected. If at a later date additional height is needed, it can be added with additional panels."

Flood protection walls and berms, walkways, trails, interpretive signage and a comfort station in the Iowa River Landing Wetlands Park on the east side of the Coralville Marriott Hotel and Conference Center was added.

"We've protected the entire city to 1 foot above 2008's flood level," Coralville City Administrator Kelly Hayworth said.

The city also worked with the University of Iowa Flood Center to create flood zone maps and plans for future flood events.

"Iowa City, the University of Iowa and Coralville all committed to using that map," Hayworth said. "We inputted our new projects into the map, so we knew what the impact would be to the whole system if we [added specific projects and flood protection measures]. It was really cool to all be able to work together and see what the impacts would be of new projects."

Floodwalls, pumps and other preventative measures were added along the Iowa River to prevent future flooding (City of Coralville).

Adding housing stock

Coralville has doubled in population during the past 30 years, in part because of its proximity to the University of Iowa and Interstate 80, as well as its abundance of shopping, restaurants and affordable housing.

A portion of that housing was lost during the flood. More than 400 residential units, mostly apartments, were damaged. Since 2008, more than 350 residential units were demolished. The city completed more than 50 home buyouts, 17 of which used FEMA funding. The buyouts were all voluntary and homes were razed. The land now serves as greenspace, sidewalks and similar uses.

About 370 new residential units have become available since the flood or are nearing completion, including:

• **Villas on 4th**, 300 block of Fourth Avenue. The former Le Chateau, which had flooded numerous times, was demolished and replaced with the Villas. The new buildings are elevated above flood levels. Flood protection is incorporated into a wall of one of the Villa buildings.

• **Riverview Plaza**, 300 block of First Avenue, built at the site of the former, flooded Briskey Cabinetry building, which was torn down. When complete in 2020, the project will include three buildings housing 124 residential units, 14,000 square feet of commercial space and a redeveloped Randy's Carpet Outlet.

• **Old Town**, from Fifth Street to Second Avenue. Includes two multi-unit buildings housing 116 residential units, 42 townhomes and 12,000 square feet of commercial space.

• **Millennium Housing Project**, 625 S. First Ave. A $68 million, five-story, mixed-use residential and commercial building is planned for the Iowa River Landing District. It will include 95 one-bedroom, 132 two-bedroom, 29 three-bedroom and 53 four-bedroom units.

Opposite: *Several apartment buildings were flooded along Highway 6 and First Avenue (City of Coralville).*

Above: *New condominiums, townhouses and apartments are filling up with tenants as quickly as they can be rebuilt (Watts Group).*

Old Town Neighborhood

A century ago, Coralville's main buildings were located along U.S. Highway 32, which later became Highway 6. Although it's been rerouted, back then, Highway 6 overlapped with Coralville's Fifth Street. Some of the town's oldest buildings are located along that stretch of road, including Old Town Hall and the 1876 Schoolhouse. During the past few decades, Fifth Street has been a centerpiece of municipal and business development, with the new city hall, fire station and library located on the west end of the road.

Clear and Biscuit creeks crisscross through the Old Town neighborhood, flooding much of that land in 2008. The area has received infrastructure improvements and been largely redeveloped since the flood. A city transit facility and the Old Town Hall were relocated to protect against future flooding.

Watts Development Group was selected to redevelop 14 acres of land at the confluence of the two creeks. The Old Town development, has 116 apartments and 42 townhomes, and includes 12,000 square feet of commercial space.

"Old Town is very successful. As soon as they've got the units built, they've been rented or purchased. They really couldn't keep up with demand," Hayworth said. "It's a good location. You can ride your bike to work at University of Iowa Hospitals and Clinics or to downtown Iowa City or wherever you were heading."

Much of the neighborhood's land that was flooded in 2008 has been converted to green space.

Plans are in place to improve sidewalks, lighting and other features of the Fifth Street thoroughfare as it leads to First Avenue and north to the Iowa River Landing District, to better connect the neighborhoods.

Opposite and above: *Old Town, one of the original neighborhoods of Coralville, was flooded in 2008. The area has become a hotspot for new residential units, shops and restaurants (Watts Group).*

Iowa River Landing District

The city of Coralville began redevelopment during the 1980s of a blighted, yet very visible part of town, at the southeast corner of Interstate 80 and First Avenue. Now known as the Iowa River Landing District, the neighborhood included several industrial businesses, including a major truck stop, towing company, salvage yard and auto-body shops.

For decades, the city bought properties in the district and razed them. In 1998, the city became eligible for several federal grants to remove the "brownfield" sites from the district, to clear the area of industrial hazards and waste. Ten years later, the city received the U.S. Environmental Protection Agency's Region 7 Phoenix Award for its work.

Today, the district is a 180-acre development with more than 330,000 square feet of retail, office, residential and entertainment space.

The Coralville Marriott Hotel and Conference Center opened in 2006 as one of the first major developments in the district and remains a popular spot for regional conferences. Mixed-use residential and commercial buildings came next, with views of the Iowa River. Among the first tenants were Backpocket Brewing's 15,000-square-foot brewery and department store Von Maur.

Development took off in earnest in 2012, when the University of Iowa Hospitals and Clinics opened a $73 million outpatient clinic in the district to help reduce traf-

Above: *University of Iowa Health Care opened its $73 million outpatient facility in 2012 in Coralville's Iowa River Landing District. Services provided range from primary care to specialties such as cardiology, dermatology and urology. (University of Iowa).*

Opposite: *Sandbags line a multiuse office and residential building in the Iowa River Landing District in 2008 (City of Coralville).*

fic at its main hospital in Iowa City. Its services range from primary care, including general pediatrics and general internal medicine, to specialties such as cardiology, dermatology, urology and women's health. The clinic serves 300,000 patients annually.

Trader Joe's opened a 13,000-square-foot store in the district in 2017, followed by women's clothier J. Jill. Ethan Allen plans to open a location there in 2019. Future plans for the district include a $46 million arena, another hotel, more housing units and additional UIHC clinics.

"I would say the IRL is moving along quicker than we expected. It's really picking up speed now. We have a number of businesses about to announce their openings in the district," Hayworth said.

In 2014, the Swift family returned to Coralville when they opened the restaurant 30hop in the Iowa River Landing. Matt Swift now owns the restaurant with Erik Shewmaker, Brian Flynn and Dan Blum. The group installed an 18,000-pound decorative rock in the restaurant, which serves American/Asian fusion and dozens of craft beers. Its rooftop patio is a popular attraction in the area.

"The Iowa River Landing is exploding; it's really filled in the past few years," Swift said. "And the restaurant is such a unique space. There's not another restaurant like it in the country. There's giant beams and the big, open feeling."

Hawkeye fans celebrate FRYfest at Coralville's Iowa River Landing District. FRYFest is a festival that kicks off the University of Iowa football season (FRYFest).

Adding green space to the river banks

Now that the bulk of the city's flood protection measures have been put into place, Coralville is working to develop more of the river banks into park land.

When the flooded homes were torn down near the Coralville Marriott, the city converted the river bank into a 5-acre wetlands park. A series of elevated walkways extend across a 2-acre pond and lead to an observation tower. Ducks, geese and butterflies are a common sight at the park, while the croaking of frogs and chirping of crickets are frequent sounds.

As additional projects and development are completed within the Iowa River Landing District, the city will add more greenspace, earthen berms and trails to the river banks. Between the district and the Iowa River Power Restaurant, the Ready-Mix concrete manufacturer will move to a new site, away from the river. That property will become park space, which will continue south along the river to Iowa City.

"Things are going to continue to improve. Both Iowa City and Coralville are really looking at the river and what we can do along the riverfront," Hayworth said. "Iowa City has the great Riverfront Crossings project and then you've got the University of Iowa and all the wonderful things they've done along their riverfront, then you come into Coralville and we've got all this greenspace and park plans and development plans. Now there's this great corridor along the river in all of our communities."

The city of Coralville has received several accolades throughout the years, including No. 59 out of Top 100 Best Small Towns 2015 and has been recognized as a most secure place to live, best green city, lowest crime city and best place to live.

The Iowa River Landing Wetlands Park, on the east side of the Coralville Marriott Hotel and Conference Center, includes flood walls and berms, walkways, trails, interpretive signage and a comfort station (Miranda Meyer).

Corridor Rising

University of Iowa

After water had destroyed so much in cities along the Cedar and Iowa rivers June 12-15, flooding continued on its path. Its next landfall was the University of Iowa, where it created the nation's worst campus flooding event in history.

"No other campus has endured a $700 million disaster. We remain the largest, independent 'customer' of FEMA," said Rod Lehnertz, UI's senior vice president of finance and operations.

The UI is a Big 10 school and Iowa's largest university, with an 1,880-acre campus and 33,000 students. Intersected by the Iowa River, the school's liberal arts campus is on the east, while arts, athletics, the medical school and UI Hospitals and Clinics (UIHC) are on the west. The 2008 flooding caused $700 million in damage to 22 campus buildings. In comparison, the 1993 flood caused $6 million in damage to campus.

As water began to overtake interstates, highways and county roads, travel throughout the state became a challenge. UIHC patients come from every county in the state for the urgent and specialized health care services available at the major academic medical center, which annually treats more than 36,000 people for inpatient care and 60,000 patients at its Level 1 trauma center. To serve that many patients, the hospital employs more than 10,000 people, who live in communities across the region, including western Illinois. To keep the hospital staffed during the flood, UIHC flew doctors, nurses and other key personnel to and from work. Planes flew twice a day between Iowa City and Cedar Rapids and between Iowa City and Moline, Illinois.

The issue of flooded roads remained fresh in the minds of officials when recovery efforts began. With so many roadways inaccessible, it became difficult for emergency responders to reach those in need. Since then, many roads have been elevated, but the issue also put added emphasis on removing homes from floodplains, to ensure residents can always be reached during emergencies.

Watching and waiting

A group of UI officials began keeping an eye on the river in early 2008. Many of them remembered damage caused by the 1993 flood – and the winter's dense snowpack offered an eerie reminder.

"We had a lot of people with experience from prior events, people who knew what to do and how to do it and we benefited from that," said Doug True, UI Health Care interim associate vice president and chief financial officer, and former UI senior vice president for finance and operations and treasurer. "We had been tested before, we knew where our weaknesses were, we knew where our key buildings and assets were."

UI officials began meeting weekly in the basement of the UI Police Department at the Old Capitol Town Center mall throughout the winter and spring to discuss ways to prevent flooding and protect the campus.

IOWA RIVER

As water levels continued to rise, those meetings became daily, with more agencies involved, such as the Army Corps of Engineers and the UI's Institute of Hydraulic Research.

The most immediate concerns were keeping utilities, such as power and water systems, operating in case of a flood.

The UI water plant, located on the Iowa River, supplies UIHC. Protective measures were taken across campus to safeguard facilities and infrastructure before the flood. Losing the hospital's water supply was not an option.

"The water plant was protected like a fortress," True said. "We protected our intakes, and the whole system over there. We made sure that, short of the whole dam breaking loose, the building would be protected."

The hospital was able to maintain its water and power supplies, remaining operational throughout the flood. Since then, UIHC has continued to experience growth and achieve new milestones. The 12-story, $360-million University of Iowa Stead Family Children's Hospital opened across the street from Kinnick Stadium in early 2017. Children and their families can watch Hawkeye football games from the hospital's top floor, and a social media suggestion launched a new

The University of Iowa Stead Family Children's Hospital opened in 2017 across the street from Kinnick Stadium. At the end of the first quarter of each Hawkeye football home game, the 70,585 fans at Kinnick turn and wave at the children watching from the hospital. The new custom received the Disney Sports' Spirit Award of 2017. (University of Iowa).

tradition. At the end of the first quarter of each home game, the 70,585 fans at Kinnick turn and wave at the children watching from the hospital. The new custom received the Disney Sports' Spirit Award of 2017.

During times of disaster, the UI partners with multiple companies, from insurance providers to contracts for sand, flood barriers and specialized cleaning crews, to protect its buildings and numerous assets.

"We hired two large, national firms for cleanup," True said. "We have them on retainer, so when we call, they come. Otherwise, you're in line with everybody else. They come in with 500-600 people and start to do the less-glamorous work that has to be done to get you functioning again. So, they went in and got all the mud out. It really put us in a good position to get them here right away."

Actual flood damage to the university was about $230 million. The rest of the $700 million flood cost came from cleanup and repairs, as well as interim solutions.

"We had 400 to 500 outside contractors on our campus at one time, going into all of the 22 damaged buildings, removing all of the drywall that was, or could have been damaged by the flood, revealing metal studs, 16-inch on center, for acres," Lehnertz said. "And then they literally, with toothbrushes, cleaned every inside and outside face of every one of those support studs. Without doing that, the spread of mold was imminent. It was an unbelievable six months of cleanup."

"THE UNIVERSITY OF IOWA PROBABLY BORE THE BRUNT OF THE FLOOD FOR IOWA CITY. BECAUSE WE'RE A BIG, STRONG UNIVERSITY, AND RELATIVELY WELL-RESOURCED, WE WERE DETERMINED AND WE DECIDED TO NOT LET IT AFFECT US IN WAYS THAT WOULD PARALYZE US,"
SAID SALLY MASON, FORMER PRESIDENT, UNIVERSITY OF IOWA.

Flooding inundated the University of Iowa's arts campus along the west side of the Iowa River, as well as many buildings along the east bank (University of Iowa).

Sandbag mountain captains and volunteers

As in other communities, volunteers spent weeks filling and placing sandbags to help protect the UI. Miles of volunteers, including students and employees, could be seen working along sand embankments across campus.

"We did not fathom how big the volunteer effort would be," Lehnertz said. "Those last couple of days, we had 3,000 people on the campus. There was this really great moment when we were gathered in that [situation room at the police department], and someone comes in and said, 'it appears we have hundreds of people walking down the street coming to help. We're going to need someone to grab a bullhorn and a golf cart and tell them where to go and what to do.'"

With school out for the year, entire families would sandbag together. Instead of their daily workouts, UI wrestlers, basketball and football players sandbagged. Residents from nearby Amish communities came to help. Future students and parents visiting campus for orientation during the flood joined the sandbagging efforts. So many people volunteered that UI officials were assigned to different "sandbag mountains" to coordinate efforts.

"We asked the UI staff to volunteer as 'sandbag mountain captains,'" Lehnertz said. "We had deans, academic directors and professors step forward before we could finish the question. And everyone dropped their title at the door."

Sadie Greiner, senior engineer and associate director for planning, design and construction for UI Facilities Management used her design expertise to create effective sandbag walls. She directed the sandbag mountain captains on how to build the walls effectively and efficiently.

On Friday, June 13, two days before the river crested, Lehnertz was at the main library sandbagging with a group of 20 volunteers. A television news crew came by and asked for an interview for the 10 p.m. broadcast.

"I gave the interview and then 20 minutes later, five trucks showed up to deliver pizzas. They had seen everybody on TV and wanted to say thanks for sandbagging," he said. "Those were some of the darkest days of my career, but far and away the most inspirational."

At midnight, Lehnertz convinced the volunteers to go home. That's when semi-truck trailers began rolling in. The trucks were carrying parts and pieces to build temporary power plant installations, as officials predicted the 1929 plant would not hold through the flood.

"We knew where the flood was going and that we wouldn't be able to maintain the main power plant," he said. "The National Guard literally had to walk the semis through closed interstate roads. At 2 a.m., our power plant operators backed out of the power plant, when it had 22 feet of standing water in it. And at that point, the campus went black."

Those same power plant operators spent the next three days working 24-hour shifts building the temporary power installations.

"Within three days, they were able to produce steam out of these makeshift power plants," Lehnertz said. "It was a critical moment in our ability to survive as a campus."

Floodwaters kept increasing every day, until the river crested at 31.53 feet on June 15, submerging campus buildings and facilities. Although the flood rose above the sandbag mountains, they shielded UI property from trees and debris coming downstream.

"It was quite amazing to see the outpouring of support we received during what were some pretty tough days," said former UI president Sally Mason, who began her UI tenure six months before the flood.

Thousands of volunteers built sandbag walls to protect University of Iowa buildings. Volunteers included students, student athletes, residents from local and surrounding communities, even students and parents on campus for orientation. Within days, the UI experienced the nation's worst campus flooding event in history (University of Iowa).

Corridor Rising

"WE HAD A LOT OF PEOPLE WITH EXPERIENCE FROM PRIOR EVENTS, PEOPLE WHO KNEW WHAT TO DO AND HOW TO DO IT AND WE BENEFITTED FROM THAT," SAID DOUG TRUE, UI HEALTH CARE INTERIM ASSOCIATE VICE PRESIDENT AND CHIEF FINANCIAL OFFICER, AND FORMER UI SENIOR VICE PRESIDENT FOR FINANCE AND OPERATIONS AND TREASURER.

Above: *Flooding west of the Old Capitol, the center of the University of Iowa campus (University of Iowa).*

Opposite: *Flooding and cleanup at Mayflower Hall (University of Iowa).*

The race to reopen

June 16, the day after the crest, was a Monday. UI officials gathered, and President Mason announced the university would be open for summer classes scheduled to begin 10 days later.

"It was important, because if we didn't do it in 10 days, we would have lost that summer and the impact on students would have been immense," Lehnertz said. "The trick was, the campus was a wreck."

Floodwaters were still higher than the Coralville Dam, so the Army Corps of Engineers continued to outflow the excess water at 20,000 cubic feet per second. Because of this, the UI remained in a flooded state for a month, until waters receded.

The focus turned to student safety and cleanup. Sandbag walls were dismantled, buildings were power-washed and academic buildings were open in time for summer classes in late June.

"I don't know how many places that had nearly $1 billion worth of damage done and were able to reopen 10 days later," Mason said.

Fall semester two months away

The UI had two months to continue to clean, repair and reopen its student buildings in time for the start of fall classes in mid-August. Because a record-size freshman class would be arriving on campus, the UI needed every residence hall operational. The reopening of Mayflower Hall, which houses 1,010 students, became a top priority. Floodwaters had surged across Dubuque Street, closing it down, and filled Mayflower with 3 feet of water. Crews worked to remove the mechanical systems from the building so the components would be dry when replacement parts arrived.

"In the midst of the flood, as we were preparing for cleanup and coming out on the other side, Mayflower was one of the first buildings flooded," Mason said. "It was clear that we didn't have a choice; if we were going to be open in the fall, we were going to need to have Mayflower open. That, and any academic buildings we would need for classes."

Cleanup and immediate repairs to Mayflower were completed in time for the fall semester. Later, in 2015, a flood wall and additional repairs and improvements were completed at a cost of $18 million.

The Iowa Memorial Union, the UI's student union with restaurants, a bookstore, student services offices and study space, is located along the river. In 2008, the ground floor took on 3 feet of water, deluging the bookstore as well as the building's mechanical and electrical systems. The IMU reopened in time for fall classes, although the ground floor remained closed for repairs. In 2015, a floodwall was added to the building with additional improvements for future flood protection. The improvements cost $39.5 million.

Nearby, the Adler Journalism, Becker Communication Studies and English-Philosophy buildings each took on 4 feet of water when the river overtook the structures and closed the adjacent Iowa Avenue. After cleanup and repairs were made, a flood barrier was installed. Improvements cost $10.4 million.

The Iowa Advanced Technologies Laboratory, an interdisciplinary building shared by chemistry, physics and engineering departments, is located along the river's edge. Several repairs and improvements were made to the building, including the addition of a 1,500-foot-long removable floodwall. The project cost $30 million.

"The University of Iowa probably bore the brunt of the flood for Iowa City," Mason said. "Because we're a big, strong university and relatively well-resourced, we were determined, and we decided to not let it affect us in ways that would paralyze us. I look back with great pride at what we were able to accomplish in spite of a lot of challenges. I remain very, very grateful to so many. We had such a strong team. It solidified my passion for the University of Iowa."

Powering up a university

Campus buildings operated without heat during summer and fall months, but UI officials set a Nov. 1 deadline for restoring operations at the power plant to warm buildings in the winter.

"If we didn't have a full and reliable steam source, we would have to shut down the campus again," Lehnertz said. "The next mad dash became drying out and replacing parts at the power plant."

Dozens of miles of cables and wires, boiler equipment and other components needed to be tested and replaced.

"On Oct. 28, President Mason blew the ceremonious whistle at the power plant to signify that it had reopened three days before the deadline," he said. "As is the theme of this flood, it was remarkable how people put in an incredible amount of time and effort to make it happen."

About $98.5 million was ultimately spent repairing and improving UI utility systems.

Opposite: *Top, the Iowa Advanced Technologies Laboratory and Iowa Memorial Union flooded; middle, the Iowa Book Store at the Iowa Memorial Union; bottom, a student exits the Iowa Memorial Union (University of Iowa).*

Top left: *Ventilating the Iowa Memorial Union after the flood; bottom, former University of Iowa President Sally Mason (center) at a ribbon cutting for several campus buildings reopening after the flood (University of Iowa).*

Corridor Rising

Arts campus under water

Without question, the hardest-hit buildings were part of the UI arts campus. Performing arts venues, the art museum, studio space, music school and theaters were overwhelmed by flooding.

Not only were audiences left without spaces to enjoy performances, but students were without practice and studio space.

UI officials were able to quickly identify and secure a vacant Menards hardware store on Highway 1, which was extensively renovated to accommodate the UI Department of Art and Art History's Studio Arts division. Campus bus routes were reconfigured to transport students to the space, which the UI ended up using for eight years.

"We created an entire arts campus in a month," Lehnertz said.

During those years, students studying jewelry and metals, ceramics, sculpture, printmaking, 3-D design, intermedia, painting and photography attended classes at the Menards building.

The new UI Visual Arts Building was completed in 2016 and includes 126,000 square feet of studio, classroom and gallery space for students. The structure has received nearly 10 national awards for its design, which

IOWA RIVER

features daylighting, a rooftop studio, thermal heating and cooling and more. The LEED Gold-certified structure cost $84.6 million.

The UI's School of Art and Art History's Art Building West is 70,000 square feet of studios, offices, classroom, gallery and library space for sculpture, painting and printmaking. The $12.8 million building, completed in 2012, also received numerous state and national design awards. Unique design elements include channel glass siding, sawtooth skylighting, daylighting and a cantilever that leads to a reading library.

The Visual Arts Building and Art Building West were designed by renowned architect Steven Holl and include extensive flood protection measures.

The UI Theatre Building also took on water, flooding its Mabie, David Thayer and Theatre B theater spaces, as well as acting studios and classrooms, design and lighting studios and prop and costume shops. Those programs were temporarily relocated until 2009 and the basement was repaired in 2014. The cost was $5.5 million.

Top left: *University of Iowa Art Building West; bottom left, an aerial view of Art Building West; top, a student navigates flood waters; left, the Studio Arts program at Menards (University of Iowa).*

161

One of the most beloved spaces on the UI campus is the performing arts venue Hancher Auditorium. Built on a hill next to the Iowa River, Hancher is one of the first sights visitors see when they travel to Iowa City. The large structure became a symbol of recovery after it flooded in 2008.

Despite its lofty perch, Hancher was in the 500-year floodplain. The river entered the building and reached the stage, destroying the building, theater equipment and seats where audiences were entertained for 36 years.

After countless community forums, officials decided to tear down and rebuild Hancher on the same lot, but outside the 500-year floodplain. Well-respected architectural firm Pelli Clarke Pelli was commissioned to design the 1,800-seat venue.

Throughout the decades, popular artists like Aretha Franklin, Bruce Springsteen and Yo-Yo Ma had performed in the space. It was the groundbreaking, experimen-

"SUDDENLY, WE HAVE THE FINEST PERFORMING ARTS HALL ON ANY CAMPUS IN AMERICA: HANCHER AUDITORIUM," SAID JIM LEACH, FORMER IOWA CONGRESSMAN AND CHAIRMAN OF THE NATIONAL ENDOWMENT FOR THE HUMANITIES (NEH), INTERIM DIRECTOR OF THE UNIVERSITY OF IOWA MUSEUM OF ART (UIMA).

tal artists from around the world, however, that made Hancher Auditorium's performances distinctive.

During its reopening season in 2016-2017, crowd favorites such as productions of "The Book of Mormon," "Mama Mia!" and "The Sound of Music," as well as comedians Steve Martin and Martin Short took the stage at Hancher. The Preservation Hall Jazz Band, which played the first performance at Hancher when it opened in 1972, was the inaugural show in the reopened space in 2016, this time featuring Trombone Shorty. Other acts included the Puppet State Theatre of Scotland, soprano Renee Fleming, dance by Step Afrika!, Inuit throat singer Tanya Tagaq and a new dance piece by Marc Bamuthi Joseph, titled "/peh-LO-tah/."

Hancher has received several awards for design, performances and diversity since it reopened in 2016. The reborn facility cost $176 million.

Opposite: *Top, the rebuilt Hancher Auditorium, and, bottom, the original Hancher under water (University of Iowa).*

Top: *Hancher Auditorium seating, and, bottom, the lobby (University of Iowa).*

"NO OTHER CAMPUS HAS ENDURED A $700 MILLION DISASTER. WE REMAIN THE LARGEST, INDEPENDENT 'CUSTOMER' OF FEMA. ALL COMMUNITIES HERE HAVE BEEN SUCCESSFUL IN THEIR FLOOD RECOVERY," SAID ROD LEHNERTZ, SENIOR VICE PRESIDENT, FINANCE AND OPERATIONS, UNIVERSITY OF IOWA.

Voxman Music Building was also completed in 2016. The UI's School of Music's former building had been connected to Hancher Auditorium before the two structures were demolished after the flood. The music program was a challenge to accommodate with temporary space, because of the acoustics needed for students to practice.

"There was no good place for music to go, so we went everywhere," Lehnertz said. "We used apartments, churches, office spaces, anything we could find for music. We did it and it created a great deal of distress in the first year, because unlike many programs, you can't have somebody practicing percussion next to a room practicing flute, in an apartment or in a church. So, we had to make changes during the year to continue to take care of music and ultimately, used the former movie theater in the Old Capitol mall."

The new, six-story Voxman connects the UI campus to downtown Iowa City and helps extend downtown south of Burlington Street. Built for $189 million, the structure includes a 700-seat concert hall, 200-seat recital hall, organ performance hall, music library, rehearsal rooms, practice rooms, classrooms and faculty studios and offices.

"The new building really rises up out of downtown," Mason said. "It took downtown Iowa City and transformed it into something that is quite special in terms of college towns around America. It's hard to imagine something more impressive or more beautiful than that particular building where it is."

Hancher and Voxman are LEED Gold-certified and have received several design and construction awards since opening.

These projects were paid for with a combination of insurance coverage, grants, donations and state and federal dollars, 60 percent of which came from FEMA. At one point, there was more than $1 billion in construction taking place for recovery projects.

Rebuilding the arts campus was essential to the UI's academic mission, Mason said.

"The arts is one of those things that distinguishes human beings from all other species on our planet," she said. "It's that appreciation for art and music and things that stimulates our creativity or innovation. I'm a scientist, so I think it's great that we have managed to turn so many young people toward careers in STEM (science, technology, engineering and math) fields. I've gotten to know quite a few scientists, whether they're biologists or engineers, who have a serious hobby or passion in either music or art of some sort. And that doesn't surprise me at all, because science and art are so closely linked."

Opposite: *The University of Iowa School of Music Voxman and Clapp buildings, flooded in 2008 (University of Iowa).*

Above: *The newly-constructed Voxman Music Building in downtown Iowa City, including the central atrium, 700-seat recital hall and acoustic reflector ceiling (University of Iowa).*

UI Museum of Art

In the days and weeks before the flood, the UI's $500 million art collection, including Jackson Pollock's iconic painting "Mural," were wrapped, loaded into trucks and transported to a warehouse in Chicago for safekeeping.

The art collection has been without a permanent home ever since.

"It is the preeminent museum in the world that doesn't have a venue of its own," said Jim Leach, former chairman of the National Endowment for the Humanities.

Since the flood, "Mural" has been attracting massive crowds as it tours art galleries around the globe. The UI's museum also houses one of the most significant African art collection in the world, as well as paintings by Kandinsky, Matisse and Picasso, among others. Much of the collection is now on display at the Figge Art Museum in Davenport.

"Mural" recently returned from a tour of European galleries and will spend most of 2018 on display at the National Gallery of Art in Washington, D.C.

"[Since the flood] we have taken on the responsibility of showcasing several of our finest pieces around the world," Leach said. "In the last three years, 1.5 million people have lined up at museums around the world to see a single painting — Jackson Pollock's 'Mural,' which is 8 feet by 20 feet and considered by many to be the preeminent piece of modern Western art."

After the flood subsided, the school's art insurer refused to cover the collection at the existing museum, which is now in the designated 500-year floodplain. Meanwhile, FEMA refused to help finance construction of a new museum, because the existing building had not experienced enough damage and could technically be reinhabited.

Below: *The University of Iowa Museum of Art flooded in 2008 (University of Iowa).*

Opposite: *Jackson Pollock's "Mural," which was rescued from the flood and is now on a world tour of art galleries (University of Iowa).*

Deadlocked after years of discussion, negotiations and appeals, the UI decided to move forward with a museum without FEMA's help. Because the university could not find insurance for the collection in the existing museum building, the institution lost its accreditation. Since plans for the new museum have been announced, that accreditation has been restored.

Work is now underway for the final piece of UI's flood puzzle. In the fall of 2017, university leaders announced plans to construct a $50 million museum next to the school's main library. The project is being led by Leach, one of Iowa's most respected statesman. He is a former Iowa congressman, UI visiting professor in law and political science and has received 14 honorary degrees. Leach is serving as the museum's interim director during the design, construction and fundraising of the building.

When complete in 2020, the new museum will house the UI's 15,000-piece collection in a 63,000-square-foot, three-story building. While the land is still in the 500-year floodplain, there will be an underground floor of parking. Art will only be displayed on the second and third floors. The museum is being designed by Rod Kruse of Kansas City-based BNIM. Kruse's portfolio includes more than 110 higher education projects and studies on 14 campuses.

"This is going to be an exceptionally efficient structure," Leach said. "We can't build a Taj Mahal, but we are going to build a very handsome museum that can be expanded. It's going to wow people, but it's not huge."

The new structure recently received a $10 million donation from Richard and Mary Jo Stanley of Muscatine, who have been longtime, generous supporters of the UI. The Stanley family developed one of the country's most well-respected collections of African art, which they donated to the museum in 1985.

As far as the existing art museum, it now houses offices and may be used as space for the dance department. Leach, who has an office in the building, has put pieces from his own art collection on the walls to spruce it up.

"THE UNIVERSITY OF IOWA HAS PROFOUNDLY BEAUTIFUL NEW BUILDINGS – HANCHER, VOXMAN, THE COLLEGE OF PHARMACY – MANY OF THOSE ARE POST-FLOOD REBUILDS. WHEN OUR ALUMNI COME TO TOWN, THEY ARE OVERWHELMED BY THE AESTHETIC OF THESE NEW BUILDINGS," SAID NANCY QUELLHORST, FORMER PRESIDENT AND CEO, IOWA CITY AREA CHAMBER OF COMMERCE; DIRECTOR OF DEVELOPMENT, UNIVERSITY OF IOWA FOUNDATION.

Learning to embrace the river

The Iowa River has experienced several smaller floods since 2008 which tested the school's new flood mitigation measures. Fortunately, none of them ever came close to 2008 levels.

Many Corridor leaders attribute the region's ability to prepare for and prevent severe flooding since 2008 to hard work, planning and improved mitigation, but also to the work of the UI Flood Center. Founded in 2009, it is the nation's first academic center devoted solely to the study of floods. The center is housed in the UI's hydraulics laboratory along the Iowa River and collaborates with groups such as the Iowa Department of Natural Resources and the National Weather Service. They work together to improve flood monitoring and prediction capabilities in Iowa. The UI Flood Center not only creates improved floodplain maps and monitors river gauges, but its engineers are creating innovative technologies. For example, a UI professor recently received a Microsoft grant to create an artificial intelligence system that will serve as a virtual flood expert, similar to Siri. The guidance provided by the flood center helps keep the region safe from flooding threats.

"We are better protected than any other campus that we know of," UI's Lehnertz said. "The presence of water and natural disasters have been and will be a part of our community. Yet the river is the most special thing about our campus and community. We had turned our back on the river since 1847, the birth of our campus. Many of our buildings' back doors faced the river. It was considered a resource for utilities, not an

amenity. While we recognize the danger of what a river can do, we have a campus that is ready for the next flood and we tested it in 2013 and 2014. It doesn't mean we're immune to the impact of floods – those are an increasing risk not just here, but everywhere. But our campus is better because of that."

After the 2008 flood receded, the UI set up a core flood team that met weekly on campus to discuss and monitor recovery efforts. In 2017, the UI retired the group after it had conducted 430 meetings. The UI now considers itself officially recovered from the 2008 flood.

"The university and the surrounding communities have all been successful in our flood recovery," Lehnertz said. "In a world where you see more extreme weather and flood risk, it makes us well-positioned to exist in an environment that would otherwise be more threatening. That has allowed us to not fear the river but to embrace it. We've done what we've needed to do to protect ourselves from the river, in order to celebrate the river."

In 2017, the UI was tied for 82nd among national university rankings, tied for 33rd among public universities, and tied for 130th among global universities by U.S. News & World Report. The same year, 16 UI graduate programs ranked among the top 25 in the nation in U.S. News & World Report. In graduate school rankings, Iowa's Carver College of Medicine tied for 25th in the country for primary care and for 33rd in the country for research, its College of Public Health tied for 17th, its College of Pharmacy tied for 17th, its College of Law tied for 20th and its Nursing School tied for 23rd.

Opposite: *The Stanley Hydraulics Laboratory at the University of Iowa, which houses the Iowa Flood Center (University of Iowa).*

Above: *Floodwalls erected around Art Building West (University of Iowa).*

Iowa City

As floodwaters overtook the UI, they also rushed into Iowa City, inundating several neighborhoods and uprooting roads, bridges and infrastructure. The river reaches Iowa City at the Normandy neighborhood, nearby City Park and across the river at the Taft Speedway neighborhood. Floodwater came over the roadway there, at Dubuque Street, and began moving toward Mayflower Hall. The water continued to rage south, pushing debris through the Park Road and Iowa Avenue bridges. Next, it ravaged the city's wastewater treatment plant and flooded part of Highway 6, as well as the Baculis and Thatcher mobile home parks near the airport, before continuing on to communities to the south. As it did in Coralville, the Iowa River crested at 31.53 feet on June 15. In 2008, the flood caused more than $160 million in damage to 1,600 acres in Iowa City.

IOWA RIVER

"IOWA CITY IS NOW BETTER PREPARED FOR THE NEXT FLOOD. OUR DECISIONS REFLECTED A SHIFT IN THINKING ABOUT THE IOWA RIVER," SAID MATT HAYEK, FORMER MAYOR, CITY OF IOWA CITY.

Flood preparations

In early June, the city of Iowa City began preparing in earnest for the flood. The Army Corps of Engineers made its initial calls to Iowa City, Coralville and the University of Iowa on June 3. That same day, the UI began sandbagging Mayflower Hall. From then on, the four groups conducted daily conference calls to stay updated on water levels upstream and on activity at the Coralville Reservoir.

"We were able to get the best information at the beginning of the day. It was a challenge, because the river was a moving target," said Rick Fosse, who served as Iowa City's public works director for 11 years, including during the 2008 floods. He joined the city as an engineer in 1989, so he was very familiar with flooding and natural disasters when the 2008 flooding hit.

Top, flood waters crash against the Coralville Reservoir (U.S. Geological Survey). Left, City Park in Iowa City is submerged. (Corridor Business Journal).

171

As the Army Corps of Engineers began increasing the outflow at the reservoir, city staff began sandbagging along Rocky Shore Drive in the Normandy neighborhood, Taft Speedway and at the mobile home parks on the south side of town. By June 5, Dubuque Street was closed, and a call center was set up for residents needing assistance.

The next day, the city held its first flood-related press conference and a local disaster declaration was signed by the mayor, as the river exceeded the flood stage. Voluntary evacuation notices were distributed to the mobile home parks, and the city's most vulnerable water wells were shut down on June 7.

At the start of the week of June 9, sandbagging was expanded to adjacent streets and neighborhoods as more roads closed. Water pumps were set up to reduce damage in those neighborhoods. The American Red Cross set up a shelter at the Johnson County Fairgrounds and the call center began receiving more than 100 calls a day.

On June 10, the Park Road Bridge at Dubuque Street, near Mayflower Hall, Hancher Auditorium and the Normandy Drive neighborhood, was closed. Crews drilled holes into the bridge to reduce its buoyancy. Water began to flow into the emergency spillway at the Coralville Reservoir.

IOWA RIVER

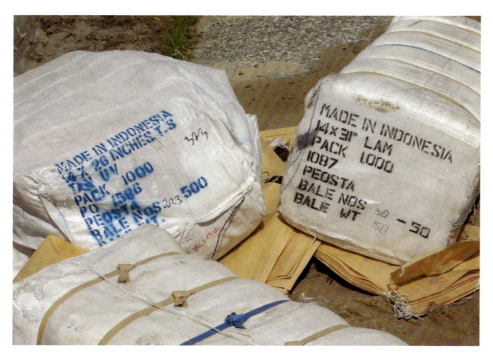

Residents and volunteers build sandbag walls to protect neighborhoods in Iowa City (City of Iowa City).

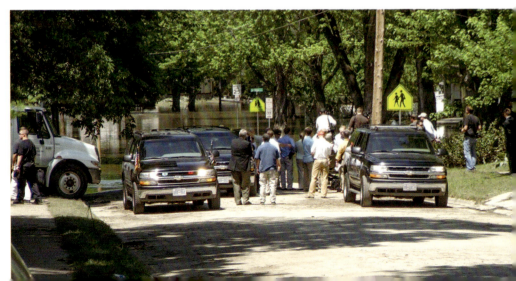

Evacuations begin

One of the more difficult local decisions was the mandatory evacuations of homes in those most vulnerable neighborhoods. The river was expected to overtop neighborhood sandbag walls on June 11.

"It was a challenge striking that balance between safety and allowing people access to their properties," Fosse said.

Heavy rains continued and conditions worsened. The city council scheduled a special meeting to discuss mandatory evacuations. Regenia Bailey, who was mayor at the time, had been in the city of Burlington for a Vision Iowa meeting, when city clerk Marian Karr called her about the meeting.

"Marian said, 'we really have grave concerns that we're going to need this [mandatory evacuations]," Bailey said. "On my way back into town, I stopped at the trailer parks and saw virtually the entire city planning department out helping residents sandbag. That was a sign to me that this was getting really serious. It was really a wake-up to the idea that this [flood] needed more than cautious watching. Now we are preparing."

Bailey and city staff toured the Normandy Drive and Taft Speedway neighborhoods to inspect the water levels.

"There were sandbag walls, people had moved things upstairs, many had been through the '93 flood. It was a neighborhood committed to riding it out and taking the flood on," she said. "Then later that evening, we decided it needed to be evacuated, that it wouldn't even be prudent to leave people in their homes until morning, the river was rising so quickly."

City Councilor Matt Hayek, who would later serve as mayor during the recovery effort, remembers the evacuations well.

"Mayor Bailey signed a late-night order requiring evacuations from the neighborhood next to City Park, and law enforcement started knocking on doors in the dark," he said. "I was dispatched to a mobile home park to use my Spanish to communicate with residents who were evacuating. I sped across town, running stoplights with my blinkers flashing, and tromped across already-soggy roads looking for anyone who hadn't yet left."

Residents were evacuated safely from homes along the river. Overall, 500 homes and 48 businesses were evacuated.

The city then focused on keeping residents and critical infrastructure protected during the disaster.

Media professionals gathered along Park Road in Iowa City as government officials surveyed flood damage (Douglas W. Jones, University of Iowa).

"IT WAS A CHALLENGE STRIKING THAT BALANCE BETWEEN SAFETY AND ALLOWING PEOPLE ACCESS TO THEIR PROPERTIES."
SAID RICK FOSSE, FORMER IOWA CITY PUBLIC WORKS DIRECTOR.

Keeping the city operational

"As we were focused on the residential effort, we were also concerned about our critical infrastructure, transportation system, water system and wastewater system," Fosse said.

The city's most productive wells are in the Peninsula neighborhood, near Taft Speedway.

"We lost that well field to the flood and our ability to produce water was significantly compromised. But fortunately, demand for water during that period of time was low," he said.

Because the city had water stored, there was only one day when there was more demand than what the city could produce.

The city was able to keep its North Wastewater Treatment Plant partially operational, enough to continue to pump water through the pipes. The facility, which was flooded, was considered a loss. The treatment plant has since been demolished and its services relocated to the city's South Wastewater Treatment Plant. Five acres of wetlands were added to the north plant site to help expand the city's flood capacity. Streambanks were restored to reduce flooding at the nearby juncture of the Iowa River and Ralston Creek.

Meanwhile, Burlington Street was the only open road allowing transportation across the river. Traffic was gridlocking, and officials worried they would need to close the Burlington Street Bridge. That move was unnecessary, but the city set up separate units of fire, police, other emergency responders and essential city services such as garbage trucks, on both sides of the river in case the bridge was lost.

"Everything was set up and ready to operate, essentially, two cities that are no longer connected with a transportation system," Fosse said.

Many city employees had worked during the 1993 flood and the 2006 tornado, learning lessons that would help minimize damage in 2008.

"That experience paid off," said Fosse, who is now a lecturer for the University of Iowa's civil and environmental engineering department, where he teaches classes on disaster planning, response and recovery.

The experience helped once again in 2013 and 2014, when the third and fourth worst floods on record hit the city. With new mitigation measures in place, damage was minimal.

"They were non-events," he said.

Cleanup and recovery

Two years before the flood, Iowa City experienced a devastating F2 tornado. One of the lessons learned from that event was debris removal. The city asked residents to put debris into four different piles on the curb. Doing so saved 25,000 cubic square feet of trash from going into the landfill. Much of it, such as tree limbs, was broken down and reused or recycled. The system also kept hazardous waste ranging from small appliances to paint out of the landfill.

When it came time to discuss future flood prevention efforts, many residents were worried that adding protection measures to one neighborhood would only worsen flooding in others. This sentiment became the focus of discussion during many community forums after the flood.

"Ultimately, what the city decided to do was to make room for the river," Fosse said. "The only true way to protect a property is to remove it from the path of the flood."

To protect against future flooding, the city completed home buyouts and is in the process of elevating Park Road Bridge and Dubuque Street. The city also removed its own facilities from the floodplain, including the North Wastewater Treatment Plant, the animal shelter and a fire department training facility.

"Unlike Cedar Rapids, Iowa City wasn't hit as hard as everyone feared," Former Councilor Hayek said. "The overall loss of homes and businesses was limited and

A worker polishes the whistle at the University of Iowa Power Plant (University of Iowa).

"OUR ECONOMY IS ALREADY STRONGER AS A RESULT OF FLOOD RECOVERY EFFORTS. NOT ONLY HAVE WE PROTECTED CRITICAL INFRASTRUCTURE, WE HAVE BENEFITED FROM PLANNING EFFORTS IN THE DOWNTOWN AND RIVERFRONT CROSSINGS DISTRICT," SAID GEOFF FRUIN, CITY MANAGER, CITY OF IOWA CITY.

our clean-up effort was manageable. The process then shifted to post-flood considerations – levies, elevation of roads, relocation of the wastewater plant and so forth. The massive infusion of public dollars and our determination to be better prepared for the next flood caused the council and staff to spend an incredible amount of time on budget and capital planning issues – raising Dubuque Street, relocating the wastewater plant, offering buyouts to eligible homes. These were massive investments in our infrastructure and required careful analysis, especially given the associated costs."

Overall, the city of Iowa City spent $159.7 million on 17 flood mitigation projects.

More than $23 million went to home buyouts, removing 101 houses from the 100-year and 500-year floodplains. The city also invested in land, so 141 houses and 22 rental homes could be built to help replace housing lost in the flood.

"Iowa City is now better prepared for the next flood," Hayek said. "Our decisions reflected a shift in thinking about the Iowa River – how it runs through town, how our riverfront amenities help, and hurt, when water levels rise, and how we can better feature the river as an attraction, yet be safe from its immense power."

Demolition and relocation of the north wastewater plant cost $55.4 million, while a new park was constructed in its place for $3.1 million. Elevation of Dubuque Street and replacement of Park Road Bridge cost $48.8 million. A lift station and flood gates at Rocky Shore Drive cost $5.4 million and a west side levee cost $5 million. Nearly $2 million was spent protecting the city's water supply. Pump stations were added to Normandy and Stevens drives for $600,000. Funding for these projects came from a number of local, state and federal sources.

Floodplain maps and hazard mitigation plans have been updated in the city to help protect against future weather events.

The flood recovery baton has been passed to Geoff Fruin, who joined the city in 2014 and now serves as city manager.

"First and foremost, we're trying to remove properties from the danger," Fruin said. "When we've had the opportunity, we've pursued buyouts. Let's let that river breathe a little bit when it needs to. That's going to be far more effective than levees and berms. Ultimately, you've got to use all those strategies, but any chance we've had, we first look at removing that structure from the floodplain."

Iowa City Gateway Project

Dubuque Street, one of the city's most essential thoroughfares, is undergoing a 10-foot elevation. The street connects thousands of homes, the University of Iowa and downtown Iowa City. Nearby roads can't handle the rerouting of its heavy traffic volume. During the flood of 1993, the road was closed for 54 days. It was closed for a month in 2008.

"Dubuque Street was our lowest and most vulnerable street and elevating it became our most important public safety project," Fosse said.

The Park Road Bridge created 14 inches of backflow during the 2008 flood, worsening the damage throughout the city. The bridge is being replaced and elevated, as well.

"The bridge becomes an obstruction for the river – it slows the water and it projects water upstream, so by the time it backs up to the Iowa River Power Restaurant, it has added a few more inches of water, worsening the flood," he noted.

The bridge had been in poor condition before the flood and the city had set aside capital funding to repair it.

"After the flood, it no longer made sense to continue to invest to repair it – we needed to replace it," Fosse said.

The two projects are being completed for $40.5 million and are expected to be finished in August 2018.

Opposite: *Flooding along Dubuque Street in Iowa City in 2008 (City of Iowa City).*

Above: *Elevation of Dubuque Street and replacement of the Park Road Bridge are expected to be completed in late 2018 (City of Iowa City).*

Riverfront Crossings

"I ANTICIPATE MORE GROWTH; WE'RE ONE OF THE GROWTH AREAS OF THE STATE. WE'VE CREATED AN ENVIRONMENT HERE THAT GIVES PEOPLE THE OPPORTUNITY TO CREATE THEIR OWN JOBS, CREATE THEIR OWN COMPANIES," SAID REGENIA BAILEY, FORMER MAYOR, CITY OF IOWA CITY.

The North Wastewater Treatment Plant had been located just a few blocks south of downtown before it was demolished and its services moved. Its removal opened an entire area for development, known as the Riverfront Crossings District. After numerous community forums and workshops, the city created a master plan for the area.

"I'm glad we did so much planning and envisioning because I think it allowed people to understand what was expected of developers, but it also gave them that picture of possibility and opportunity," former Mayor Regenia Bailey said. "I think that really helped. It was a very public process. There were a lot of community conversations and that created a lot more excitement around it. It was also about public policy changes, to make sure people didn't live in danger because we knew it would happen again. We learned as we went and maintained a lot of transparency and access to citizens."

The new district is bordered on its north side by the UI's Voxman Music Building, a new hotel, MidWestOne Bank's new, six-story, Class-A office building, apartment buildings, 600-space parking ramp and expanded county offices. To the west, it is bordered by Riverside Drive on the west side of the Iowa River. The eastern border is Gilbert Street and the southern border is Highway 6. More than $160 million has been

invested in the pedestrian-friendly area since 2013 and at least another $100 million in investment is expected.

The city of Iowa City has moved ahead with phase one of a 17-acre park, which will be used as a recreation area and double as flood mitigation greenspace. Ralston Creek, which flooded in 2008 and runs through the district, is being restored and additional wetlands and trails are being added as part of the project.

The park was the selling point for the Swift family, who opened its Big Grove Brewery & Taproom in the district in March 2017. It is the eighth restaurant for the family, which was convinced it would leave the restaurant business after the 2008 flood. It's the second Big Grove location; the original Big Grove Brewery opened in Solon in 2013.

"I really love the idea that Big Grove was born in the flood of 2008, we just didn't know it yet," Matt Swift said.

The Swifts had been looking for a property in downtown Iowa City for its next Big Grove location, and the park at Riverfront Crossings put all the pieces together.

"Once you're facing the creek, that's the nature tie-in to Big Grove," Swift said. "Big Grove was a township of Solon, named that because it was a big grove of trees. So, to have the nature tie-in at the Iowa City location was crucial."

Big Grove Brewery & Taproom is in the former UI Surplus building at Highway 6 and Gilbert Street.

Apartment buildings are going up and park land is going in at Iowa City's new Riverfront Crossings District, just south of downtown (Angela Holmes)

"Specifically for Big Grove, we wanted to be near downtown," Swift said. "We thought it was important that it develop into part of the university experience and be part of the Iowa City experience. And to do that you have to be centralized near downtown. Being walkable and bikable was really important. To find this opportunity was pretty special."

The 28,000-square foot building was completely remodeled and has become a hotspot, popular for its craft beers, live music and games.

Several other businesses are making plans to open in the district, many citing the new park as the attractor. What was once blocks of industrial facilities has become greenspace, commercial, residential and offices.

"The park is really transformational for the properties around there," Fruin said. "It's a signature park within the city and you're starting to see businesses that are recognizing the city's investment there. They want to be a part of it. You get a business like Big Grove that not only opens up but chooses to do so in a way that faces the park. Traditionally, businesses would have their entrances on their street side. Big Grove really focused their building to embrace that park and to bring that parklike atmosphere into their business."

Iowa City typically receives several accolades for its quality of life each year. Its locally-owned downtown bookstore Prairie Lights was named a Top 10 Bookstore by National Geographic, for example. In 2018, the city ranked No. 4 on Livability's Top 100 Places to Live. In 2017, it was named a best place to retire, best city for entrepreneurs, one of the coolest cities in America, best small metro to live after college graduation, best mid-size city for most volunteers by corporation and came in at No. 5 among best college towns in America.

Above: *Nine years after Slugger's Neighborhood Grill flooded in Coralville, the Swift family opened Big Grove Brewery in Iowa City, along the Iowa River (Angela Holmes). Popular for its live music, bar games and craft beer, Big Grove is an anchor of the Riverfront Crossings District.*

Cedar and Iowa rivers join at Columbus Junction

Floodwaters continued to move south through Hills, where it damaged farmland and to Wapello, where a levee was destroyed. Before the Iowa River joins the Mississippi River, it runs through the 171-person town of Oakville. In 2008, the town was completely submerged. Every one of the town's homes and businesses was flooded and remained so for 10-14 days. Ninety percent were a total loss. But as Mayor Benita Grooms and FEMA began community conversations about the future of Oakville, many decided to stay and rebuild. More than 35 percent of housing has been rebuilt and more than a dozen businesses have come back. Today it calls itself, "The Little Town that Would Not Drown."

The Iowa River emptied into the Mississippi River, where railroad bridges had washed out in several places, locks and dams were damaged and barge traffic slowed. Eventually, the flooding lessened as it worked its way toward the Gulf of Mexico, leaving an enduring mark on the communities along the way.

Above: *Columbus Junction residents Janice Pugh, Frieda Sojka and Cathy Crawford made the long walk up Highway 92 ramp after delivering homemade lunches to the Iowa National Guardsmen manning the roadblock to the flooded road. (Greg Henshall, FEMA).*

NONPROFITS

African American Museum of Iowa

55 12th Ave. SE, Cedar Rapids
blackiowa.org

When the African American Museum of Iowa took on more than five feet of water during the flood of 2008, it found itself in the same boat as other area museums that needed to clean and preserve their most valuable items.

Then known as the African American Historical Museum and Cultural Center of Iowa, the museum at 55 12th Ave. SE, Cedar Rapids, sustained $1.3 million in damage. Sitting next to the Cedar River in between the New Bohemia District and Czech Village, the building's entire main floor was severely damaged.

While the carpet, walls and fixtures could be easily replaced, the museum's exhibits, documents and artifacts required unique professional attention to be saved.

The museum joined forces with several other nearby flood-damaged centers – the National Czech & Slovak Museum & Library and the Johnson County Historical Society – and the University of Iowa Libraries and the State Historical Society of Iowa to salvage their collections.

The group selected disaster recovery company Steamatic, of Alsip, Illinois, which lowered administrative overhead costs by sharing the company's staff and equipment.

Although many of the African American Museum of Iowa's one-of-a-kind photographs were damaged beyond repair, 1,000 photos that survived triage, 200 textiles and 15 works of art were sent to the Chicago Conservation Center. Overall, 90 percent of items were salvaged.

Dry items were housed in the Iowa Masonic Library and Museum at 813 First Ave. SE, Cedar Rapids, for storage during the six-month restoration process.

While Federal Emergency Management Agency (FEMA) funds were minimal, "much of the recovery costs were afforded by grants, state programs and individuals," said current Executive Director LaNisha Cassell.

To prepare for future natural disasters, adjustments were made to the building's layout including making the permanent exhibit easily movable, storing paper-based archives higher and allocating additional loft storage space in the event items needed to be moved to higher ground.

The improved disaster plan was tested in September 2016 when the Cedar River rose to just above 22 feet – the second highest crest in recent history.

"We were attentive to what was happening in 2016 when we saw the predictions," said Brianna Kim, director of operations. "We enacted the emergency plan, which includes tiered priorities for evacuation. Our collection is the first tier, and all objects were moved above six feet."

The power of social media also played a key role in 2016 as volunteers came out in droves.

"We had such a great turnout from the community, we were able to send some volunteers to other venues to assist," Cassell said. "We learned more lessons in 2016 and were able to update our emergency plan even more."

The exposure through social media has increased traffic at the museum, especially from out-of-town visitors as well as patrons of the Czech Village/NewBo Main Street neighbors.

"So many people have a connection to African-American history across the state," said Krystal Gladden, museum educator. "Access to this shared history is what the African American Museum of Iowa provides on a daily basis."

Sponsored by:

Left: *Contents of the museum's first floor were destroyed and discarded (African American Museum of Iowa).*

Cedar Rapids Public Library

450 Fifth Ave. SE, Cedar Rapids
www.crlibrary.org

Through early June 2008, Cedar Rapids Public Library staff watched the Cedar River rise, virtually across the street from 500 First St. SE.

"We were keeping an eye on the river gauges leading up to that awful week, but I don't think anyone had an idea it was going to be as severe as it was," said Kristine Olsen, then a reference librarian and now a materials librarian. "We didn't have any real prep time to even begin to do what was necessary."

"It happened so fast, and it happened so violently," said Susan McDermott, then and now a member of the library's board.

Shelved books absorbed moisture and swelled, bursting their spines and eventually bursting the shelves.

"It was just devastating," said McDermott, named to the library's board in January 2007. "That building had been the result of a lot of hard work to get something that really fit the community. It wasn't that old, and we were so tremendously proud of it."

As a rule of thumb, about a third of a library's collection is checked out at a time. The library began rebuilding its collection around those books while recovery and rebuilding continued. Temporary operations were established at Westdale Mall and a small downtown facility.

"It was extremely challenging," Olsen said. "We had virtually no space in the beginning, so we were practically working on top of each other."

A west-side satellite library opened in February 2013 at 3750 Williams Blvd. SW.

The Federal Emergency Management Agency (FEMA) funded the in-kind replacement of a public building: no additions or improvements. And FEMA wouldn't fund rebuilding the library at its pre-flood location.

"That's important for people to remember," McDermott said. "When they said that, we knew we had to look at other buildings."

That led to 450 Fifth Ave. SE, then the home of TrueNorth. The board worked out a property swap with the insurance company, which moved into the old library, eliminating its first floor space for parking.

The new library needed to catch up with nearly 30 years of cultural and technological change. The Cedar Rapids Public Library Foundation raised the money for the improvements beyond an in-kind replacement.

The new building overlooking Greene Square Park opened

in August 2013. Circulation has boomed from pre-flood levels.

"It was a sad time and then it became a frustrating time, then it became a great time," McDermott said. "It went full circle, and the community came out of it. I don't know any other town where people take visitors to the library but that happens all the time. And I don't think many people have weddings at a library, but they do here."

Sponsored by:

Above: *Floodwaters inundated the downtown library, destroying much of its collection. (Cedar Rapids Public Library) The new facility opened in 2013 (Knutson Construction).*

Four Oaks

5400 Kirkwood Blvd. SW, Cedar Rapids
www.fouroaks.org

Like many other community service organizations, Four Oaks staff members found creative ways to continue operations immediately after the flood. Numerous employees worked out of their homes, their cars or doubled up in spaces at Four Oaks' facilities that had not been impacted by the flood.

A canoe was even employed to get to the former Hayes Elementary School on D Street SW – the site of the organization's community-based programs – where staffers were mucking out the building.

Four Oaks, along with affiliate organizations including the Jane Boyd Community House and the Affordable Housing Network in Cedar Rapids and Family Resources in the Quad Cities, serve approximately 30,000 at-risk children and families. The majority live in Cedar Rapids.

During the flood, the immediate concern was for the children and families living near the Cedar and Iowa rivers, according to Anne Gruenewald, president and CEO of Four Oaks.

"We had to evacuate about 12 children living in our shelter and residential treatment facility in Iowa City to our site in Independence," Gruenewald said. "Because of road closures, we had to drive them to Des Moines, then to Mason City and down to Independence. What normally would have been an hour trip took about five hours."

In addition, a huge challenge for social workers was locating and following families, including adoptive and foster families, who lived in the flood plains. Many had to leave their homes and were living with family, friends or in shelters. In some cases, people eventually moved away from the community.

At the same time, Four Oaks – with expertise in a number of areas including crisis care and housing – was asked by the city of Cedar Rapids to serve on several flood response committees.

Through this committee work, partnerships formed with government and community groups became much more structured, according to Liz Mathis, community engagement director.

"The various groups learned from one another and learned how to streamline project management and cut through bureaucratic red tape," Mathis said. "As a result, the city is not only better prepared to respond to future natural disasters, but it's also in a better position to continue ongoing sustainable work to improve and strengthen distressed neighborhoods."

Mathis said one area that has benefitted from lessons learned from the flood is the Wellington Heights neighborhood in southeast Cedar Rapids. Working with the Wellington Heights Neighborhood Association and the Cedar Rapids Police Department, more than 100 problematic house properties in an 18-block area were identified, purchased and renovated. Occupancy density in these houses has been reduced and single-family home ownership has increased.

"It's contributed to increased safety and stability of families in the neighborhood," Mathis said. "And it's just one outgrowth from the flood recovery efforts."

Sponsored by:

Above: *Four Oaks worked with the city of Cedar Rapids to repair homes in the Block by Block program (Four Oaks).*

Hawkeye Area Community Action Program (HACAP)

1515 Hawkeye Drive, Hiawatha
www.hacap.org

On a typical day, approximately six employees at the Hawkeye Area Community Action Program (HACAP) answer the 2-1-1 phone line for the United Way of East Central Iowa. The 2-1-1 service connects callers with local agencies that can provide them with needed resources.

The days immediately following the historic flood in June 2008 were anything but typical, and the HACAP facility in Hiawatha became an information hub for the city of Cedar Rapids. The phone system in the building on Hawkeye Drive was turned into a 2-1-1 call center staffed 24/7 by countless volunteers.

According to Jane Drapeaux, chief executive officer of HACAP, the organization also took over the Cedar Rapids city call line, providing citizens with critical information including when they could safely go back to their homes and inspect their properties.

"In addition, our Hiawatha facility became a center for a host of city, county, state and federal employees working to support the flood response operations," Drapeaux said.

HACAP also played an essential role in the disaster recovery efforts in Linn, Johnson and Benton counties. According to Mitch Finn, deputy executive director, many low-income residents served by HACAP lived in flood plain areas.

"The federal contracts that enable us to assist these individuals and families give us flexibility to use the resources for disasters like the flood," he said. "For instance, we were able to employ home evaluators from our weatherization program to assist in the initial evaluation of home property damage."

"HACAP is about meeting needs and building strong communities," Drapeaux added. "This was a time to step up and pour our resources into helping flood-affected individuals and families."

HACAP serves six counties in Eastern Iowa in the areas of food and nutrition, homelessness, energy conservation, veterans assistance and children's support.

One program that has been growing in the years following the 2008 flood is the Operation BackPack program, a partnership between HACAP, schools and communities. It serves elementary school children with food insecurity issues in their homes.

Volunteers pack nutritional, child-size foods in bags for children to take home and eat over the weekend. The program serves approximately 3,000 children in 72 schools located in the counties served by HACAP.

"The BackPack program is supported by funds raised locally, and Diamond V – headquartered in Cedar Rapids – is a huge supporter," Drapeaux said. "Having adequate food to eat is critical for these children. They're not able to think, pay attention to the teacher or participate in classroom activities when they're distracted by growling tummies. This program helps fill the food gap so they can be successful in school."

Sponsored by:

Below: *Diamond V employees help pack food for children to take home over the weekend for HACAP's Operation BackPack program (HACAP).*

NONPROFITS

Matthew 25

201 Third Ave. SE, Cedar Rapids
www.hub25.org

Matthew 25, an independent nonprofit organization, had been operating for just two years when the Cedar River exceeded its banks in historic proportions in June 2008.

The organization was serving the Taylor Elementary School area in southwest Cedar Rapids with a mission "to help people strengthen their neighborhoods by focusing on safe, affordable housing, healthy food and quality education."

When the flood occurred, Matthew 25 had just two half-time staff people – founders and brothers Clint Twedt-Ball and Courtney Ball. The two quickly responded not only to those living in the Taylor School neighborhood, but expanded the organization's focus to include the flooded Time Check neighborhood in northwest Cedar Rapids.

"First, we knocked on doors to see if people were okay and to begin helping them through the mourning process," said Twedt-Ball, executive director of Matthew 25. "We asked them what they needed and then sprinted to try to bring them as many resources as possible to begin rebuilding."

The home rebuilding effort evolved into the Block by Block program, a collaboration of Matthew 25, the Four Oaks program Affordable Housing Network and the Iowa Conference of the United Methodist Church.

In the program, people who lived on a block drove the redevelopment of it. Sixty percent of the residents in a block had to sign up to participate, commit to regular meetings and help fix up their houses.

"People needed to have the opportunity to have a say in what they wanted to have happen on their block, and they were willing to work long, hard days to rehabilitate their homes and revitalize their neighborhoods," Twedt-Ball said.

More than $6 million in funding for Block by Block came from federal, state, local and private sources. Approximately 200,000 volunteers from all over the world contributed more than a million hours of work to the program.

From July 2009 to February 2012, approximately 25 blocks and 270 homes were rehabilitated. Block by Block has since been recognized statewide and nationally as a model for disaster recovery and neighborhood revitalization.

As a result of the program, the staff at Matthew 25 grew to 20, learning about strategic planning and putting effective systems in place to tackle big issues.

The staff is using that knowledge in several new programs, including Transform, an initiative that recruits volunteers the last week in June to support west-side homeowners with home repairs and improvements.

Another program is a two-acre urban farm on G Avenue NW that features a greenhouse and outdoor kitchen and teaches kindergarteners to adults about growing and preparing fresh produce.

"From the flood, we also learned about the value of neighbors and their energy in driving progress," Twedt-Ball said. "We continue to try to capture that going forward."

Sponsored by:

Left: *The Block by Block program created by Matthew 25 helped Cedar Rapids neighborhoods recover (Matthew 25).*

National Czech & Slovak Museum & Library

1400 Inspiration Place SW, Cedar Rapids
www.ncsml.org

Now bigger and better than before the flood with a more prominent presence in Cedar Rapids' Czech Village neighborhood, the National Czech & Slovak Museum & Library could have easily gone elsewhere.

"We looked at a lot of sites around town, but we ended up staying a few hundred yards away and 11 feet higher," said Gary Rozek, chairman of the museum's board in 2008 and '09.

"We did keep a totally open mind on where we would go," said Sue Olson, board chair in 2010-'11. "We solicited input from the community, and I use the term community broadly – we're a worldwide institution."

In the week before the Cedar River's June 13 crest, staff and volunteers moved as much as they could – two semi-trailers' worth – from the riverside museum.

"The whole city was certainly not in denial, but certainly unaware there was anything as brutal on the horizon for us," said Olson, who helped pack. "I remember thinking to myself, 'Well, this is good exercise, and in a few days we'll do the reverse and be done.'"

But when staff returned six days after the crest, "the horror of it was mind-numbing," he said.

An October 2008 board retreat resulted in short, medium and long-term plans. First, staff and supporters would let the public and government officials know they intended to rebuild. Medium-term meant operating out of temporary locations while the long-term solution – a new museum building – was pursued.

In addition to state and the Federal Emergency Management Agency (FEMA) funds, a recovery campaign drew more than $6 million in private donations and 10 million Czech koruna (crowns) – about $600,000 – from the government of the Czech Republic. Some of the Czech aid went to the Cedar Rapids Sokol society and the city's public library.

"They wanted to support the whole city, in addition to the museum," said NCSML President and CEO Gail Naughton, who is retiring in June 2018.

Hundreds turned out on June 8, 2011, to watch the 1,500-ton building begin its move at a pace of inches a day. It took all summer to move it 480 feet west and raise it to allow a parking garage to go underneath.

When it reopened the following July, the museum had 50,000 square feet of floor space, up from about 20,000 square feet in two buildings.

The institution's new philosophy is as important as the building, Naughton said.

"We have made a significant focus on serving the community, especially children and families," she said. "This was not the greatest strength of ours before the flood, but today I would say it is our greatest strength."

That helps the museum routinely draw more than 50,000 visitors a year, compared to about 30,000 annually pre-flood.

"We persevered and got it done," Rozek said.

Sponsored by:

Above: *Since being renovated and relocated, the National Czech & Slovak Museum & Library has hosted many community events (John Richard).*

Orchestra Iowa

119 Third Ave. SE, Cedar Rapids

www.artsiowa.com/orchestra

The Cedar Rapids Symphony Orchestra wasn't in a good place in early 2008.

"The orchestra was on its way to its own self-destruction" when the flood hit, said Tim Hankewich, Orchestra Iowa's music director who joined CRSO in 2006. "Inefficient, expensive and it wasn't leading to artistic outcomes. It was not a place that was pulling together in the same direction. In many cases we were still operating as though it was the 1970s."

"Orchestras all over the country were struggling," said Tim Charles, then the orchestra's board chair. "Many still are. We needed to position ourselves to capture a larger audience. It was tough to do that."

Hankewich, Charles and others were working on those issues but progress was slowed by a natural resistance to change and internal politics. The flood changed all that, introducing a new urgency.

The flood all but destroyed the orchestra's home, the Paramount Theatre, which had undergone a $7 million restoration just five years earlier. Headquartered next door, the orchestra's losses also included its entire subscribers list.

"Our subscriber base was now anonymous to us," Hankewich said. "We had to start from scratch. For a month, Robert (Massey, then the orchestra's CEO) and I were running the orchestra with smartphones. In a matter of weeks we had to redesign an entire season that (usually) takes a year and a half."

Emergency brought opportunity, forcing decisions that had been debated for years. Scrambling to find a new venue before the fall, Hankewich and Massey were offered Coe College's Sinclair Auditorium. But the orchestra's audience was usually too large for a single Sinclair performance, and consecutive open dates weren't available.

The orchestra looked south to Iowa City's West High School, and "an entire Iowa City symphony series was created," Massey said. "It would have taken five years if the flood hadn't taken place."

With other performances added at Independence, Elkader, Fairfield and Mason City, the expansion in its reach led to the Orchestra Iowa name.

"The most difficult, controversial change," Hankewich said of the broader reaching name. "If we were going to perform around the state, our name needed to reflect that. The hardest thing about making the transition was that people thought we were going to be abandoning Cedar Rapids."

The city asked board member Jim Hoffman to oversee Paramount's eventual re-restoration, which included $4 million in acoustic improvements and other features.

"We redesigned and rebuilt the theater," Hoffman said. "Today, I would describe it as one of the nicest performing arts spaces in the Midwest."

And Orchestra Iowa?

"It's certainly more stable than most of its peers," Hankewich said. "We are much more diversified, artistically and financially. I think we've pretty much recovered. I wouldn't want to go through it again, but the flood was the best thing that ever happened to us."

Sponsored by:

Below: *The flood seriously damaged Orchestra Iowa's headquarters as well as the Paramount Theater next door (Orchestra Iowa).*

Theatre Cedar Rapids

102 Third St. SE, Cedar Rapids
www.theatrecr.org

If Theatre Cedar Rapids' (TCR) 2008 flood experience was performed on stage, it would depict the resilience of a theater company and a multitude of volunteers in overcoming a devastating natural disaster to come back bigger and better.

More than 50 feet of water filled the 1928 building on First Avenue and Third Street in downtown Cedar Rapids, filling the sub-basement and basement before rising almost four feet above the stage in the first-floor auditorium.

When the flood waters receded, TCR staff and board members undertook the emotional task of surveying the enormous damage. They also lived up to the famous saying, "The show must go on."

The Cedar Rapids Opera Theatre was preparing to open a show at TCR and found an alternative location for its production. TCR's "High School Musical" was re-staged and performed a few short weeks after the flood at the Linn-Mar High School auditorium. The final summer show, "Gypsy," was presented at McKinley Middle School.

Meanwhile, the former Plaza movie theater at Lindale Mall was rented and transformed into TCR Lindale in time for the 2008 fall theater season. The Linge family of Cedar Memorial made the former Turner Mortuary funeral home available for temporary office space and several other theater functions.

And then there was the recovery of the downtown building. TCR had just launched a capital campaign for some modest building upgrades. When storefront tenants on the north side of the building decided not to return after the flood, the vision of the campaign expanded, according to J. David Carey, finance and administrative director.

"We had the opportunity to reclaim the entire building for TCR and improve the volunteer and audience experiences," Carey said. "Money raised from the capital campaign assisted with the matching dollar requirement for a Vision Iowa grant, and we also obtained funds from the Federal Emergency Management Agency (FEMA)."

In February 2010, "The Producers" opened in the multi-million dollar renovated theater building, making it one of the first private organizations to reopen downtown, according to Pat Deignan, Cedar Rapids market president of Bankers Trust. Deignan was president of TCR's board of directors at the time of the flood and now serves as a trustee.

"We wanted to be one of the first to reopen our doors to show that downtown Cedar Rapids was back," he said.

TCR's vision to return bigger and better has come to fruition, added Katie Hallman, executive director of the theater company.

"The community showed us that TCR is important to them," she said. "About 55,000 people came through our doors last year for live theater and classes. In addition, we have about 3,000 volunteers. It's an inspiration to us to continue to be bold in our arts offerings and our economic contributions to the city."

Sponsored by:

Above: *TCR staff and supporters showed their resolve to rebuild after the flood (TCR).*

The Arc of East Central Iowa

680 Second St. SE, Cedar Rapids

www.arceci.org

In 2008, floodwaters ravaged the first floor of the building at 680 Second St. SE in downtown Cedar Rapids with more than eight feet of river and sewage water, resulting in hundreds of thousands of dollars in damage and lost programming supplies.

The Arc of East Central Iowa, which occupies space on two floors of that building, serves people with intellectual and developmental disabilities in a seven-county area. It offers a number of specialized services, including teaching basic life skills, respite for caregivers and daycare and after-work enrichment programs.

In 2008, the organization was serving approximately 800 consumers, many who lived in the Cedar Rapids metro area, according to Jody Bridgewater, director of services and support.

"Our consumers range in age from infants to older adults," Bridgewater said. "Many families depend on our skilled services so parents can work. It was challenging, but we were able to continue most of our services with little interruption, thanks to the awesome work of the staff and the support of the community."

Almost immediately, many organizations and businesses offered space in their buildings for temporary staff operations and a couple of the daycare programs, including Regis Middle School, Christ Episcopal Church, Cedar Hills Community Church, St. Andrew Lutheran Church, Creative Software Services and REACT, a former Rockwell Collins facility.

Bridgewater also credits an outpouring of financial support for allowing The Arc to return to its downtown facility so quickly. Staff returned to the second-floor office space just five months after the flood. The Arc reclaimed first-floor space previously leased to the Girl Scouts, enabling it to expand several services and place all the programs under one roof at the downtown facility. The remodeled first floor reopened in April 2009.

"Hundreds of people and numerous corporations and businesses stepped up to help us," she said. "A number of our Arc families held garage sales and bake sales. And one of our consumers, Tyler Smothers, organized a 'Tour de Flood 2008' fund-raising bicycle ride."

Smothers, who was born with a rare form of spina bifida, pedaled a challenging three laps around Cedar Lake on his adult adaptive bicycle. His efforts raised more than $15,000 to help rebuild The Arc – a place he cares deeply about.

According to Kyle Schramp, senior director of operations, Smothers' bike ride was just one way the community gained a better understanding of how The Arc serves those with special needs.

"One positive outcome of the flood is that there's more awareness about how critically important we are to the people we serve," Schramp said. "As a result, we've gained increased support from the community which has benefitted The Arc in so many ways."

Sponsored by:

Below: *The Arc building took on more than eight feet of river and sewage water during the flood of 2008 (Arc of East Central Iowa).*

United Way of East Central Iowa

317 Seventh Ave. SE, Cedar Rapids
www.uweci.org

The United Way of East Central Iowa's response to the flood of 2008 is a prime example of how the organization connects groups and individuals to help a community in need.

"It's what the community expects of us during a difficult time," said Leslie Wright, UWECI vice president of community building.

Housed in the basement of the Kirkwood Resource Center at 1030 Fifth Ave. SE on the outskirts of downtown Cedar Rapids in June 2008, UWECI was spared the flooding that impacted places like Mercy Medical Center just a block-and-a-half away, allowing staff to jump right in to help coordinate the long recovery process.

UWECI assisted on-the ground organizations like Serve the City to immediately dispatch volunteers to needed areas. As the initial cleanup progressed, the focus turned to long-term recovery.

The Linn Area Long Term Recovery Coalition (LALTRC) was formed in July 2008 to mobilize the collective resources of businesses, funders, nonprofits, faith communities and local and state government. UWECI played an active role in the LALTRC, making connections with organizations and forming new relationships.

"One of the blessings is that we have a lot of networks," Wright said. "United Way's role was sending out the invitation, setting the table. We connect and multiply."

Since the formation of LALTRC in 2008, more than 70 organizations have worked together to bring more than $20.5 million in resources and services to Linn County, resulting in more than 600 reconstruction projects.

UWECI was also involved the Community Recovery Center which served as a one-stop shop for flood survivors who needed help above and beyond Federal Emergency Management Agency (FEMA) funds. At one time, the organization administered 17 funds, aiding in much-needed relief for families who had nowhere else to turn.

While the magnitude of the disaster came with many challenges, UWECI was able to fine-tune and expand its operations with the experience.

"The biggest impact on us was the organization had to turn inside out," Wright said.

When the 2008 flood hit, UWECI employed a half-time volunteer coordinator and operated a website. After the flood, it added Sue Driscoll, who heads a team of three full-time employees.

The problem-solving skills and relationships established during the 2008 flood continued in September 2016, when the Cedar River rose to just above 22 feet – the second highest crest in recent history. A strong network of volunteers and invaluable lessons learned from 2008 limited the damage in 2016.

"The generosity of spirit really shows up when we need each other," Wright said.

UWECI moved into the new Human Services Campus of East Central Iowa at 317 Seventh St. SE, Cedar Rapids, which opened in 2010.

Sponsored by:

Above: *Volunteers from General Mills help the United Way of East Central Iowa (UWECI).*

Waypoint-Madge Phillips Center Shelter

318 Fifth St. SE, Cedar Rapids

www.waypointservices.org

While floodwater circled the Waypoint and Madge Phillips Center buildings along Third Avenue SE in Cedar Rapids, it didn't appear to have entered the two buildings, giving staff members false hope.

Upon entering the facilities, they discovered several feet of sewage water in the lower levels of both buildings. Furniture and washers and dryers were among the items destroyed. Hygiene products, diapers and other supplies collected for individuals and household families in crisis were lost.

Although the buildings had to be closed for cleanup and renovation, hundreds of people still needed the emergency homeless shelter, domestic violence and child care services provided by the Waypoint-Madge Phillips Center.

At the time of the 2008 flood, the Waypoint building sheltered victims of domestic violence, while an emergency homeless shelter was available at the Madge Phillips Center, according to Carrie Slagle, managing director of critical services.

"Those in our shelters who didn't have family or friends they could stay with temporarily were connected with Red Cross emergency shelters," Slagle said. "Our domestic violence and sexual assault crisis line was rolled over to a cell phone so we could continue to answer calls 24/7."

In addition, the preschool and school-age child care programs had to be relocated. The preschool children were transitioned to nearby St. Paul's United Methodist Church. The summer camp for the school-age children was moved to Erskine Elementary School.

"The mindset among staff members was, 'We can do this,'" Slagle said. "We rolled up our sleeves and went to work finding ways to continue our services to those in need while getting our facilities operational again."

The Waypoint-Madge Phillips Center campus reopened in the fall of 2008. Rather than returning to business as usual, the staff took the opportunity to strategically plan for the future. After examining nationwide data and trends, a key change was made in the assistance offered to victims of domestic violence.

"The data revealed the majority of domestic violence victims don't need a shelter. Rather, they need more comprehensive services like safety planning, accompaniment to court to get no-contact orders, and medical and legal advocacy support groups," Slagle said. "We can serve many more victims in this manner."

As a result, the Waypoint domestic violence shelter was closed, but the one at the Madge Phillips Center is available. Waypoint also uses hotel vouchers and partners with other homeless shelters to help victims with temporary shelter if needed.

"A silver-lining to the flood is that it did provide an opportunity to evaluate and enhance our services," Slagle said. "And it showed that even if we don't have a facility to operate out of, we will find a way to help those in need."

Sponsored by:

Above: *Although floodwaters didn't reach the Wayoint buildings, several feet of sewage water destroyed many items (Waypoint).*

Cedar Rapids Metro YMCA

207 Seventh Ave. SE, Cedar Rapids
www.crmetroymca.org

Bob Carlson remembers standing on the railroad embankment about a half-block from the Helen G. Nassif YMCA the day before the Cedar River crested.

"I was standing over here on the railroad tracks early that morning, and I could see the water was going to come over the sandbags," said Carlson, then and now president and CEO of the YMCA of the Cedar Rapids Metro Area.

The area Y's flagship building at 207 Seventh Ave. SE was just six years old in 2008. Operations ceased about noon that day, June 12. Volunteers and staff placed sandbags around the building – not high enough to prevent inundation, as it turned out, but still a useful effort.

"That kept that mudslide from rolling into the premises and mitigated our damage by a couple of million bucks," said Mike Sheeley, chairman of the YMCA board in 2008. "It didn't keep the water out, but it kept the mud out."

Still, water filled the building eight feet, seven inches deep, destroying gymnasium floors and flooding the pool. Staff re-entered the building June 17.

"It switched from mitigation to resolve," Sheeley said of staff and board priorities. "We are going to get this back up and going."

"It was just 'go' mode," Carlson said. "I said to the board and the staff together, 'I don't know what I'm doing, but we're just going.' We looked at the best possible solution at the time, and we moved forward."

The widespread disaster complicated recovery fundraising, Sheeley said.

"The thing that made it challenging for all the nonprofits was, if you had had an isolated event like the YMCA burns down, then the city can rally around," he said. "But when you've got hundreds screaming 'we need help' at the same time, you've got to pick and choose your battles."

The YMCA's recovery was supported by the Hall-Perrine Foundation and individual donors. Included was more than $200,000 from YMCAs across the country.

The organization directed its 10,000 members to satellite locations until the Nassif building's second floor – housing offices, the main gym and track – reopened in mid-August. Full operations resumed about a month later.

The YMCA now has a disaster plan, which went into operation in September 2016 as the river neared its second-highest crest.

"We went back to the plan," Carlson said. "We were all sandbagging. (Water) never got there, so it was a big deal how that worked."

Besides a working plan, the flood left a big impression and confidence in staff and volunteers' ability to cope.

"The resiliency of everyone, that was the biggest word I can use," Carlson said. "The staff and volunteers, we had an incredible number of people that came out of the woodwork to help us, from preparing to recovery."

Sponsored by:

Below: *Community members volunteered to sandbag the Cedar Rapids Metro YMCA building before the flood hit (YMCA).*

SMALL BUSINESS

Office Express

207 Second Ave. SW, Cedar Rapids
www.officeexpress.us

About a week and a half after the flood of 2008, Randy Keel and Kathy Moeder were finally permitted to enter the site of their family business, Office Express, at 207 Second Ave. SW, Cedar Rapids. But they didn't stay long.

After being overrun by floodwater, the building and its contents were lost. Three months later, the structure was torn down.

It was a difficult time for Keel and Moeder, siblings who grew up in the family business. Their father, Dick, purchased the building in 1982 for his pharmaceutical business. Keel started a copy paper division in that location in 1986, and it eventually expanded into a business-to-business company offering a full line of office products. It became known as Office Express in 1998.

In spite of the emotional connection to the building, Keel said there was no time to feel sorry for themselves.

"We had to move forward and not dwell on what had happened," he said. "There were 17 people working at Office Express when the flood occurred, and we decided we were not going to let any employees go. We were all in this together."

The day before the Cedar River crested at 31.12 feet, employees moved as much of the office contents off the floor as possible and packed up computers. Keel grabbed essentials to keep the company going and left with what he described as "the business in a box." Operations were set up in Keel's home, where trucks arrived from 2-3 a.m. to deliver products.

"We didn't miss a day of business," Moeder recalled. "Our customers remained loyal and stuck with us. And we had a lot of clients who were also displaced by the flood and needed supplies for their temporary operating spaces. We couldn't stop. We had to keep the business running."

The Office Express operations were later moved from Keel's home to a small office in a warehouse on Rockford Road SW. Eventually the decision was made to rebuild on the family-owned property at Second Avenue SW.

On July 1, 2010, employees moved into the newly constructed building. On the wall in Keel's office hangs a photo of his father that he was able to rescue just before having to evacuate in 2008.

"We are home," Moeder said.

Since the flood, Office Express has continued to grow. It now has 22 employees, including a third generation of the Keel family. The company has clients in each of Iowa's 99 counties and in all 48 contiguous states.

"I think the lesson is to never give up," Keel said of the re-

covery process. "Keep going. Keep moving forward and come back bigger and better."

Sponsored by:

Above: *The Office Express building was torn down due to flood damage (Office Express).*

Simmons Perrine Moyer Bergman PLC

115 3rd Street SE, Suite 1200, Cedar Rapids
www.spmblaw.com

Simmons Perrine Moyer Bergman PLC (formerly Simmons Perrine) has been located in the U.S. Bank building at 115 Third St. SE in downtown Cedar Rapids since the building opened in 1929. At the time of the flood of 2008, the firm occupied floors 10-12 of the building. The firm suffered no flood damage, but the building was not accessible and had no utilities.

Fortuitously, the firm bought BlackBerry cell phones for its lawyers and many staff in February 2008. Because of the new equipment, communications among lawyers and clients proceeded very well during the flood.

The Evacuation

On Wednesday, June 11, the board of directors made the decision to start evacuation. Office Administrator Cheyrl Hines served as the main line of communication to staff and attorneys during what they believed would only be a few days of displacement. "We packed up the server and planned to be out a few days," said Hines. The servers were moved to the Iowa City office, so communications and the network were inaccessible for only a few hours. Unfortunately, the hope of a quick recovery and return to the building did not happen.

On the first Saturday following the flood, the bank allowed temporary access to the building for two hours. The firm hired a truck and swarmed the building with lawyers and staff to grab necessary files and supplies for the duration of being out of the building.

Keeping Business Moving

The board held a company-wide meeting, conveying a message of motivation and hope. "We wanted the firm to continue running, even under the extreme circumstance, and assured our staff there would be no lapse in pay and everyone would continue having work to do," said Roger Stone, the managing partner.

At first, the staff tried to run the firm administration from Hines' home in Mount Vernon. When they learned the return to the building would be delayed, the firm needed a longer-term solution. The firm then moved operations to Mount Vernon's middle school which was vacant due to summer break. Although daily business was conducted in classrooms with tiny student desks and chalkboards, the firm never lost its focus on serving its clients.

Coming Home

The U.S. Bank building was the third building in downtown Cedar Rapids to come back from the flood, reopening July 17. Although the building's power was run on a generator and only one elevator worked, the employees were grateful to be home. "When people returned, they didn't worry about petty things; they were just happy to be back," Hines said. "The experience brought everyone closer together and created stronger relationships."

The emergency situation also exposed the need to update the firm's technology, which proved to be priceless when the Cedar River rose again to flood levels in September 2016. "Technology today allows for easy communication and the ability to work remotely," commented Hines.

When flood levels rose in 2016, SPMB was displaced for a week, but did not have any disturbances in workflow because of these new technologies.

In hindsight, the firm's pre-planning, good luck, and experienced administration helped make the best of a bad situation. The six weeks of going back to middle school was a spirit building activity. Through everyone's hard work and dedication, the firm's business and client service continued without a hitch.

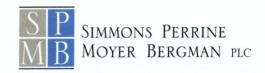

Above: *The Cedar River floods the streets of downtown Cedar Rapids (Don Becker, U.S. Geological Survey).*

Sponsor Index

Alliant Energy	36
Bankers Trust	88
Capstone Charity Resources	61
Cedar Rapids Bank & Trust	96
City of Cedar Rapids	31
City of Coralville	124
City of Iowa City	170
CRST	90
Diamond V	48
Greater Cedar Rapids Community Foundation	57
King's Material	51
Kirkwood Community College	64
Knutson Construction	100
NextEra Energy	21
Physicians Clinic of Iowa, PC, (PCI)	98
Ryan Companies	92
TrueNorth Companies	86
United Fire Group	82
University of Iowa	150
Van Meter	45

An artist performs in front of the Cedar Rapids Museum of Art (Calcam AP, LLC).

Footnotes

Photo Credits

Alliant Energy, Bankers Trust, Baxa's Sutliff Store and Tavern, William P. Buckets, Calcam AP LLC, City of Iowa City, City of Coralville, City of Cedar Rapids, Cedar Rapids Public Library, Corridor Business Journal, Brian Draeger, Federal Emergency Management Agency (FEMA), FRYFest, Greater Cedar Rapids Community Foundation, Greg Hall, Cindy Hadish, Greg Henshall, Angela Holmes, Jeff Holmes, Douglas W. Jones, King's Material, Kirkwood Community College, Linn County, Miranda Meyer, NextEra Energy, Orchestra Iowa, Paramount Theatre, PCI, Don Poggense, Ryan Companies, John Richard, TrueNorth, United Fire Group, University of Iowa, U.S. Geological Survey, U.S. Government Publishing Office, Van Meter Inc., Watts Group.

Footnotes

NOAA National Centers for Environmental Information (NCEI) U.S. Billion-Dollar Weather and Climate Disasters (2017). https://www.ncdc.noaa.gov/billions.

Linhart, S.M., and Eash, D.A., 2010, Floods of May 30 to June 15, 2008, in the Iowa and Cedar River basins, eastern Iowa: U.S. Geological Survey Open-File Report 2010–1190, 99 p. with appendixes.

Federal Emergency Management Agency, Mitigation Assessment Team Report: Midwest Floods of 2008 in Iowa and Wisconsin; Building Performance Observations, Recommendations, and Technical Guidance, FEMA P-765, October 2009.

GO Cedar Rapids, 2017, GO Cedar Rapids 2017 Official Guide.

Community Impact: Flood 2008 Report, The Greater Cedar Rapids Community Foundation, October 2011.

Guzman, Thomas, "Report of Findings/2008 Flooding in Iowa Communities," Rebuild Iowa Office – Economic and Workforce Development Task Force, August 2008.

"Central Iowa Floods of 2008," U.S. Department of Commerce, May 2009.

Zogg, Jeff, "The Top Five Iowa Floods," National Weather Service WFO, Des Moines, Iowa; March 2014.

Advanced Hydrologic Prediction Services, National Weather Service, www.weather.gov.

National Research Council. 2012. Disaster Resilience: A National Imperative. Washington, DC: The National Academies Press. https://doi.org/10.17226/13457.

"Draft Environmental Assessment: City Hall and Community Center Relocation, Palo, Iowa," U.S. Department of Homeland Security, May 15 2009.

"The Kirkwood Index," Kirkwood Community College, July 2008.

Robinson, Dennis P., "Regional Economic Impacts of the 2008 Flood," May 17, 2010.

Linn County Board of Supervisors, "Moving Forward: Our Progress During Recovery, Linn County Annual Report 2009," Dec. 21, 2009.

Schnepf, Randy, "Midwest Floods of 2008: Potential Impacts on Agriculture," Congressional Research Service, July 16, 2008.

Bloss, Bob, "Cedar Rapids-based TrueNorth re-energized by trading downtown locations with library," Rough Notes Co., May 2012.

Corbett, Ron, Beyond Promises, Big Fox Publishing: North Liberty, 2017.

Fowler, Sandi, "Flood Management and Rebuilding Plans Help Iowa Town Recover," GovTech, Aug. 26, 2009, http://www.govtech.com/featured/Flood-Management-and-Rebuilding-Plans-Help.html.

Tate, Eric; Strong, Aaron; Kraus, Travis; Xiong, Haoyi; "Flood recovery and property acquisition in Cedar Rapids, Iowa," Natural Hazards, Feb. 2016.

The Cedar Rapids Area Chamber of Commerce, "First Business Case Management Program for a Natural Disaster: Cedar Rapids, Iowa, June 2008 Flood," Jan. 2012.

OPN Architects, online work portfolio, http://opnarchitects.com/work.

"Fiscal Year 2017 Annual Report," Cedar Rapids Public Library, http://www.crlibrary.org/about-us/annual-reports.

City of Cedar Rapids, "Other Social Effects Report, City of Cedar Rapids, Iowa - Flood of 2008," June 7, 2010, www.cedar-rapids.og.

Save CR Heritage, "Historic Smulekoff's Building Opens for Bids in Downtown Cedar Rapids," March 1, 2015, https://www.savecrheritage.org/smulekoffs-opens-for-bids.

Czech Village and New Bohemia Main Street District, "History of the District," http://crmainstreet.org/history-of-the-district.

Brucemore, "The Sinclair Family," www.brucemore.org/history/people/sinclair.

Save CR Heritage, "Summit Tours Shine Spotlight on Historic Buildings," July 31, 2014, https://www.savecrheritage.org/summit-tours-shine-spotlight.

"Sutliff Bridge: Sutliff's Ferry Bridge," HistoricBridges.org, http://historicbridges.org.

"Sutliff Bridge," National Park Service: National Register Digital Asset System, https://npgallery.nps.gov/AssetDetail/NRIS/98000520.

Sayre, Robert F., "Learning the Iowa River," The Iowa Review, 39.2 (2009): 98-133. web.

"Iowa Falls Bridge," HistoricBridges.org, http://historicbridges.org.

Phares, Brent M.; Dahlberg, Justin M.; and Burdine, Nicholas, "Implementation of a Pilot Continuous Monitoring System: Iowa Falls Arch Bridge" (2015). InTrans Project Reports. 126.

U.S. Army Corps of Engineers, "Coralville Lake," undated, http://www.mvr.usace.army.mil/Missions/Recreation/Coralville-Lake/About-Us.

Johnson County Historical Society, "Coralville Old Town Hall," undated, https://johnsoncountyhistory.org/coralville-town-hall.

Hancock, Jason, "Highways of Iowa City," Iowa Highways, 2015, http://www.iowahighways.org/highways/iowacity.html.

Coleman, Jenn, "Iowa River Landing: Rethink, Rebuild, Renew," Coralville Connection, Winter 2011-2012.

Rossiter, Molly, "'Air taxi' was critical to hospitals during 2008 flood," Iowa Now, Sept. 2, 2016, https://now.uiowa.edu/2016/09/flood-profile-uihc-team.

Fosse, Rick, "2008 Flood Incident Chronology," 2008.

Anderson, Leo "Jace." "Oakville Mayor Fights to Save Town," Federal Emergency Management Agency, May 21, 2009, video and transcript, https://www.fema.gov/media-library/assets/videos/73588.

Thank You

We would like to thank everyone involved in the making of this book – especially those of you who shared your stories and photos. The 2008 Midwestern U.S. Floods left an indelible mark on the entire Corridor. The experience is one we will always carry with us in our hearts and minds.

Everyone at the Corridor Media Group was affected by the flooding of 2008. Some of us were deeply affected, others of us less so. As a business, we took on water just two weeks after moving into our new office space at Coralville's Iowa River Landing District. No one was injured and the damage was minimal, but we all remember the water, the mud, and working for weeks in the publisher's basement.

During the next several years, the Corridor Business Journal produced thousands of articles chronicling the flood, its damage and recovery. All of the greatest stories in history start with an insurmountable challenge – but they never end there. This book aims to spotlight and preserve not only the progress and improvements since then, but the unparalleled strength and grit shown by the people of the Corridor, in the face of such an epic weather event. We hope this book captures the incredible neighborhoods, community spaces and business projects borne out of the 2008 floods.

The Corridor Business Journal staff celebrated the grand opening of its new office at the Iowa River Landing in Coralville just two weeks before the area was flooded in June 2008, destroying office materials and brand new carpeting (Corridor Business Journal).